IMAGES
of America

CHINESE IN TEHAMA COUNTY

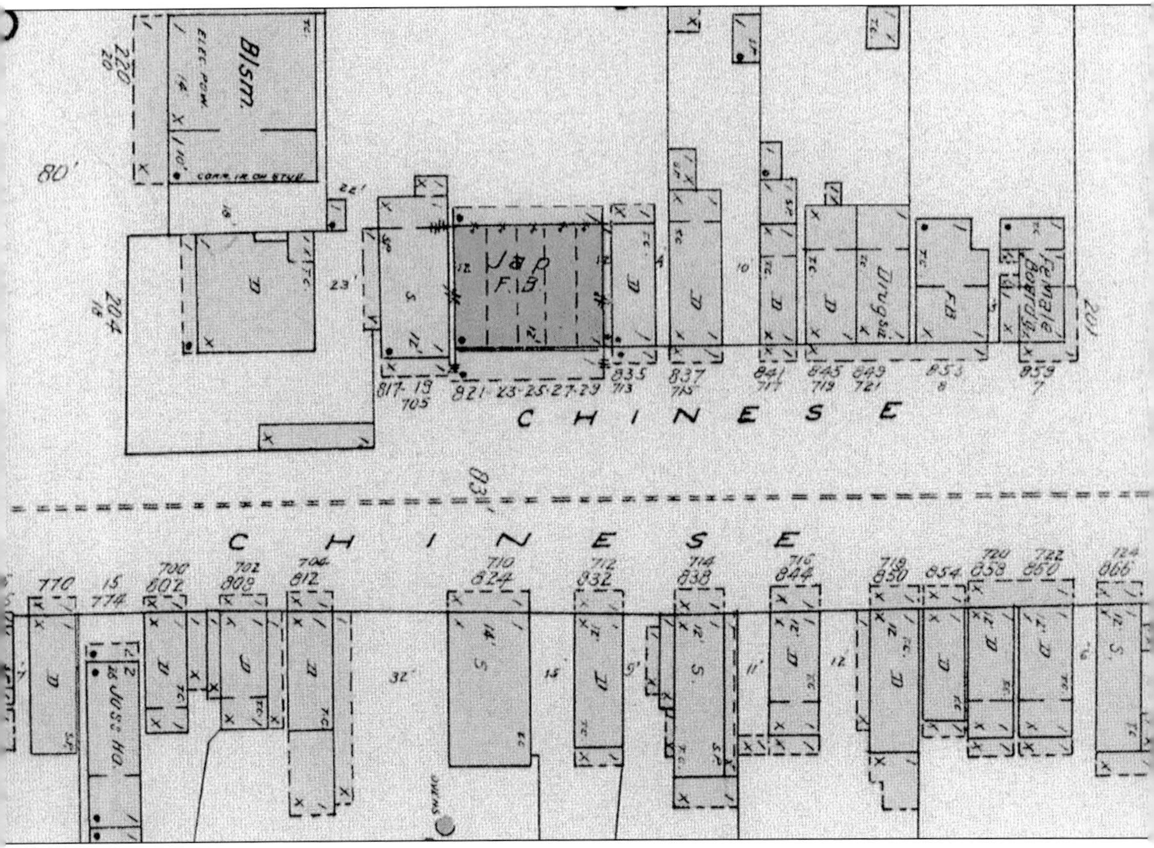

This Sanborn Fire Insurance Map of Red Bluff, Tehama County, California, will serve as a reference for the stories of a segregated neighborhood called Chinatown (today known as Rio Street) between Hickory and Pine Street in 1912. The Sanborn Map Company considered Chinatown a highly hazardous area because of the wooden dwellings. Property owners such as O.A. Lovett, B. Hearson, and the Ward and Cox families leased property to Chinese immigrants. (Library of Congress.)

On the Cover: Red Bluff, California, had the longest-reigning Chinatown in Tehama County, beginning before 1852 and existing until World War II. On the left, Joe You Chew became the longest-living Chinese American to ever reside in Tehama County. On his right is his niece Julia Chew at their family's first restaurant, called the California Café, located at 619 Walnut Street, Red Bluff, California. Unless otherwise noted, all images contained herein are from the Chew family.

IMAGES
of America

CHINESE IN TEHAMA COUNTY

Helen and Joe Chew Foundation

ARCADIA
PUBLISHING

ISBN 978-1-4671-6144-2

Published by Arcadia Publishing
Charleston, South Carolina

Printed in the United States of America

Library of Congress Control Number:

For all general information, please contact Arcadia Publishing:
Telephone 843-853-2070
Fax 843-853-0044
E-mail sales@arcadiapublishing.com

Visit us on the Internet at www.arcadiapublishing.com

This is our homage to the 19th-century Chinese pioneers of Tehama County.

Contents

Acknowledgments 6

Introduction 7

1. 19th-Century Pioneers of Tehama County 11
2. Angel Island Immigration Process 49
3. 20th-Century Chinese American Descendants 63
4. Chinese American Veterans 85
5. Cantonese American Funeral Processions 99

About the Organization 127

ACKNOWLEDGMENTS

This book is a testament to the deep love of Joe Chew's only grandchild, who was inspired by his wisdom to organize, preserve, and document his life's journey, sparking the descendants to work together as their ancestors once did. We extend special thanks to the descendants who generously shared their origin stories, memories, and experiences for this book, and whose collections of photographs were remarkable, though some were chosen to meet the publisher's requirements. The private collections of Russell and William Wong Foey (who are the last Foey and On descendants to reside in Tehama County), Bob Fong, Robert Fong, Janet Chan, Bruce Chin, Wei-ling (Yuen) Louie, and the Chew family were invaluable in making this book.

This book follows the naming conventions of the time, with individuals presented by their surname first or by the name of their business, along with women referred to by their husbands' names rather than their own given names, reflecting their community identity.

We are grateful to those who worked tirelessly to touch the lives of future generations of Asian Americans. Special thanks to the community of Tehama County, Humboldt Asians & Pacific Islanders in Solidarity, Tehama County Museum, Tehama County Genealogical and Historical Society, Colusa County Historical Society, and the Tehama County Library for unlocking a special time in history. We thank Georgia Scott at the Tehama County Library for digitizing the *Red Bluff Daily* newspaper.

Unless otherwise noted, all images contained herein are from the Chew family.

INTRODUCTION

The lands of Tehama County attracted many different ethnicities for emerging agricultural communities and later gold mining districts, specifically in Mount Shasta. Before California's statehood in 1850, it was common in Tehama County to become naturalized citizens of Mexico to obtain land grants. For those who settled in Tehama County, the main appeal was its many modes of transportation, beginning with the steamboats reaching 384 miles from the headwaters near Mount Shasta to the Sacramento-San Joaquin Delta. It was the furthest point north the steamboats could travel on the Sacramento River, once called the "Nile of the West" because of its excellent channel for inland commerce. By the 1860s, Tehama County was thriving with emerging towns where riverboats churned.

When gold was discovered in 1848, many people around the world traveled to California hoping for a better life, leading some to the last steamboat stop in Red Bluff. During this time, people in China were solicited to work abroad so that they could strike it rich by finding gold in 金山 (Gum Saan, which translates as "Gold Mountain" or "California") and use their riches to improve their village, fund educational institutions, obtain land for expansion projects, and more. The New World was promising after years of natural calamities, floods, lack of education, and economic and social instability. When the 金山客 (Gum Saan Haak, which translates as "travelers to the Gold Mountain") arrived in each town around the world, they would establish what is referred to as a Central Business District (CBD), comprised of merchants, laborers, farmers, and other trades necessary for economic success. However, there was a misconception that once you made it to America, life would be easier. Due to growing Chinese animosity across the United States of America, the Chinese community was often segregated to live in undesirable areas called Chinatown and buried in segregated sections of cemeteries. With strong Confucian values, the 金山客 (Gum Saan Haak) persevered and would diligently take any savings from their American earnings, sending them to their family remaining in China, and such funds were not for a single household, but rather to be divided among the families as outlined in a letter. The 金山婆 (Gum Saan Po, which translates as "Gold Mountain wives") prioritized paying for their son's Confucian education, food, fabric for making clothes, and, if any remaining funds permitted, other luxuries. Under the assumption that families were receiving money from the overseas workers in the 金山 (Gum Saan), some villages had young men on watch guard in towers to warn citizens of raids by bandits, kidnappings, and ransoms for money. For the overseas Chinese workers, their journey led to globalization, with some first landing in the 金山上末班車 (Gum Saan Dai Fow, which translates as "Great City of the Golden Hill" or "San Francisco"), then traveling on another steamboat to the head of navigation, and the last ferry stopped in 雷德布拉夫 (Red Bluff, California). Near the ferry stop, streets were lined with bustling Chinese merchant stores beginning on Pine Street with the first crossroad as High Street (currently known as Rio Street), and just one block further west would become Main Street, where the old US Route 99 West meets 99 East. For the 金山客 (Gum Saan Haak), their arrival would require them to travel in groups on foot or by wagon to mitigate attacks by anti-Chinese white laborers as they voyaged to different job sites. They would rest a few days in what is known today as Red Bluff's Historic District, which is where the Chinese community was segregated to live, and the area on record was called Chinatown. The landlords of the Chinese community would be Joseph S. Cone, O.A. Lovell, B. Hearson, Arthur L. Conrad, and Kraft, Ward, Cox, and other Caucasian families. Upon arrival, for those from 台山 (Toisan or Taishan) China, Tehama County had many similarities, such as alluvium clay-like soil, which, for some, made farming difficult to cultivate. However, the Chinese community liked the soil along the river and planted gardens alongside, selling produce to the entire county. Overall, the familiar terrain made it easy for the Chinese community to implement many successful ancient civilization innovation methods in the young primitive country.

Some of the earliest Chinese people arrived with their employers, settling throughout Tehama County in various business ventures. In 1857, Maj. P.B. Reading was considered a luxury for having stalks of Chinese sugar cane, and many citizens patronized three Chinese washhouses. By 1861, F. Phillips of Oak Grove commercialized Chinese sugar cane by selling syrup, a cultivation technique that had been developed in China during the Tang Dynasty of 640 AD.

Maps from 1889 depicted Corning's Chinatown on the outskirts, located on Solano Street between Fourth and Fifth Streets. Most Chinese laborers were from the Wong clan, with occupations as farmers and cooks who lived at men's boardinghouses. Others lived with their employers, such as Ed L. Sandford, Gustave and Dora Lissch, Charles Gallagher, Michael and Mary O'Neil, and John and Alice Marchant, as well as James and Elizabeth Howell.

Chinatown in Vina, California, was located on Seventh Street between Railroad Avenue and D Street. Sam Lee owned a home with a ground lease from Rosina Frese. In 1844, Peter Lassen and General John Bidwell were among the first to obtain Mexican citizenship for the purposes of owning land. Their 59,000-acre ranch in Vina, California, was later purchased by Senator Leland Stanford, becoming the Great Vina Ranch, employing Chinese immigrants to work on the world's largest winery of the nineteenth century.

Whereas in contrast, in the City of Tehama, Chinatown was centrally located on D Street next to the Tait House, W.P. Mathews building, city hall, John Simpson's Hardware store, Wells Fargo, the Postal Telegraph Company, Opera House, Heider House, E.W. Storrs saloon, John Cavalier's barbershop, and Charles Nangler's shoe shop.

Nationally, in 1862, there was much debate regarding discouraging Chinese immigration, but this same community was where taxes were mainly collected from, and the newspapers were circulating the best "mode and manner of getting rid of the vast influx of Chinese, which if not speedily checked, threatens to overrun our State." Tehama County records show they collected over $17,000 from Chinatown's property taxes, with Quong You Low Company paying as much as $1,999 in 1902. Thereby, Tehama County benefited tremendously by supporting these thriving neighborhoods that contributed so much to the economic development of their towns. According to the 1860 US Census, most of the population in Tehama County's Chinatowns was underreported because the residents thought they were evading the tax collector.

By the end of 1862, the great flood occurred, sweeping away indiscriminately settlers' properties and causing great damage in Washington, Oregon, California, Nevada, Utah, Arizona, and New Mexico. During this period, many structures were adobe. The Chinese community in Tehama County was disproportionately affected because they primarily lived in wooden structures, and many drowned. Some towns had become a sea for up to three months, and others were lost and never rebuilt. Most towns responded to the great flood by building over the first level of the town with landfill, raising their overall elevation, and some buildings were constructed with subterranean basements, which today are plagued with folklore of Chinese tunnels. According to Frances Leininger and Eleanor Simpson Briggs's research, the 700 block of Main Street in Red Bluff is thought to be the second level of the town. Another major flood occurred in 1881, but this time, it destroyed Tehama's Chinatown and drowned several Chinese residents.

By 1878, town leaders such as Wendell Phillips were not shy about supporting the Chinese community, even telling the popular newspaper *Daily People's Cause* "that the Irish, who only fifty or thirty years ago came here and took shelter under institutions already established, should use the rights we have shared with them to oppress and torment the Chinese, is shameful inconsistency, another instance of how often the persecuted are themselves the first to persecute. Shame on the Irishman who, after his country's four centuries of protest and rebellion, borrows of England the self same infamous and hateful weapons to use them against the Chinese." Others would continue to comment, stating, "It is not the fault of the landowners nor the present tenants (of Chinatown). . . . White men and their families will not go to those districts . . . offer them a garden, rent free, and not one in twenty would attend it. . . . But while you are berating men for renting to the Chinese because White men don't want to become tenants and while you are cursing the Mongolians for accepting and paying for what the white man wouldn't have as a gift, just remember men who don't want to work deserve lecturing as well as the Chinaman, who has to go and tend the peanut field because other men won't do it. Be reasonable." When incidents occurred where 50 men or so reportedly forced the Chinese workforce from the Rock Creek mining areas, the town frowned upon their malicious mischief. Overall, Chinese opposition in Tehama County was mostly from a small population of Irish citizens and a few agitators rather than the majority of the town's merchants, who supported the Chinese community by providing testimonials for their immigration.

Dr. Chew Yuen became well known within the county for hosting annual dinners to merge the cultures and even addressed the American audience by saying, "The Chinese laborers ask nothing more than their daily bread in exchange for the manual labor they perform, and many would be glad of the opportunity to render this service to the United States during the war, and by giving these people the opportunity of rendering this service would be an unlimited gain to the United States during the labor shortage. I sincerely hope this plan can be carried out not alone for the benefit of the Chinese but also for the benefit of the farmers of California." Dr. Chew's leadership would create a unique legacy of union between the Chinese community and white merchants.

The Mineral Lodge, located in Mineral, California, favored hiring Chinese chefs for their popular coffee shop serving American comfort food, due to their polite demeanor and reliable coverage. Jo Ann Perkins recalled, "They never departed work without a replacement." While Chinese cooks prepared American comfort food, they would celebrate with traditional dishes of roasted duck, whole pig, and the classic favorite, thousand-year-old duck egg.

These are the origin stories of Chinese Americans during a time when Tehama County had the most central mode of transportation.

One

19th-Century Pioneers of Tehama County

From the 1860s through the 1880s, the workforce in Tehama County was predominantly Chinese, who were the largest immigrant population. The Chinese workforce formed close-knit communities with burial areas and traditional ovens. Fellow Chinese dignitaries shared the responsibility of sponsoring big Chinese New Year festivities in their respective Chinatowns. Each of the Chinatowns in Tehama County was successful from the start, with the City of Red Bluff particularly reigning the longest due to its central location to most modes of transportation, acting as Northern California's regional center for business. There were five original Chinese American families who settled in Red Bluff, California. The 黄 (Wong) clan was the largest population throughout Northern California and one of Red Bluff's first pioneers, Wong Foey (Wong Duk Shun) from Tin Sum village (田心村), Sha Tin District. In 1862, Wong mined for gold, then worked as a hotel keeper, took on a role as a Chinese foreman for Occidental Lumber Company, and managed the Kraft Orchard on Thomas Creek. The second family to settle was the 趙 (Chew) family, arriving in 1865 as physicians to the Chinese community, establishing the Bo Do Hong Company headquarters with the 劉 (Lew) family. The 趙 (Chew) family created numerous Traditional Chinese Medicine (TCM) practices throughout the United States and overseas. Additionally, the 趙 (Chew) family became known for its Chinese American banquets in Red Bluff for the end of the Gregorian calendar year. Soon after, in the 1860s, the 鄺 (Fong) clan arrived with the T.H. Ramsay family in Battle Creek, California. The 陳 (Chin) clan was the last family to settle in Red Bluff. The Chinese community was proud of its work in America and even replicated Western brick building designs and integrated railroads in their respective villages in China.

After US Route 99 was created in 1926, Tehama County was still widely accessible to each of Tehama County's Chinatowns.

Throughout Tehama County, the Chinese community negotiated their wages at $1 per day, and it was customary for their compensation to include their housing and meals. Pictured is the world's largest winery of the 19th century, located in Vina, California. Leland Stanford hired a significant number of Chinese workers. (Department of Special Collections, Stanford University Libraries.)

The Chinese community worked as cooks and farmed English walnuts, pecans, chestnuts, oranges, lemons, pomelos, figs, peaches, pears, prunes, and apricots on Stanford's ranch. In 1886, Stanford hired 300 Chinese seasonal farmers to pick grapes. By 1887, the Chinese community went on strike for higher wages at Stanford's ranch. Today, the land has been subdivided, but the pomelos still thrive. (Department of Special Collections, Stanford University Libraries.)

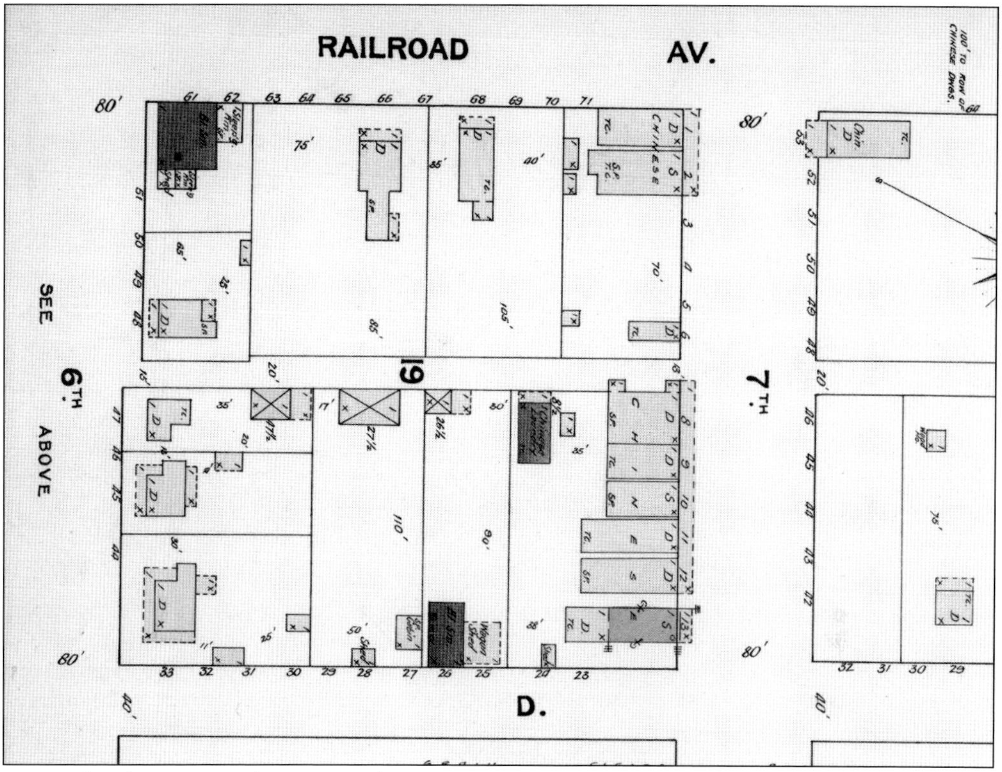

Pictured is the 1893 Sanborn map of Vina. When the Geary Act of 1892 was implemented, only 75 Chinese residents reportedly registered in 1893. By 1906, Wing Lock Hong operated the Chinese Masons in Vina, paying a monthly rent of $2 to landlord R.H. Reno. (Library of Congress.)

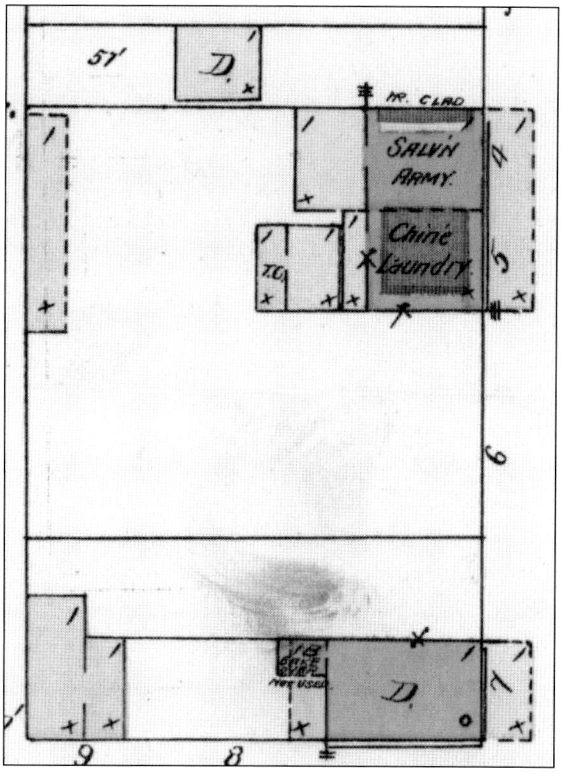

Through multiple partnerships, the most successful businesses with the lowest upfront capital were gardens and laundry services. Pictured is the 1900 Sanborn map showing the largest Chinese laundry business in Tehama County, located on Main Street, where Sacred Heart Church is today in Red Bluff. (Library of Congress.)

In the early years, Red Bluff's Chinatown was once the major supplier of produce for all of Tehama County. This is a picture of Julia Chew in the garden for the Ming Terrace Restaurant, the last surviving garden and restaurant owned by one of the original Chinese American families who settled in Red Bluff, California.

The US Census Bureau undercounted most of the Chinese community in Tehama County. After the 1892 Geary Act was passed, many blamed the Chinese merchants, who catered largely to Chinese customers, for encouraging laborers not to report their residency status. Pictured on the right is SH Loy Kee General Store, located at 802, and on the left is 803 High (now Rio) Street, Red Bluff.

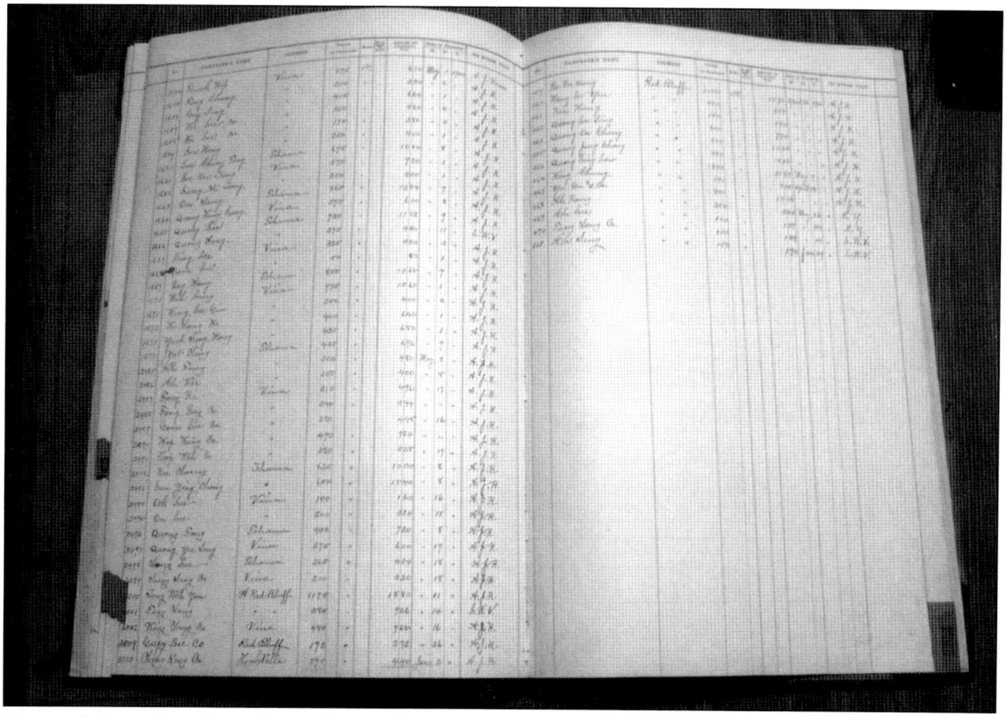

Pictured here is a long list of annual property taxes collected throughout Tehama County's Chinatowns. By 1870, the Foreign Miners Tax paid by the Chinese community contributed almost a quarter of California's revenue of more than $5 million on top of property taxes. Since the Chinese community had no ability to be recognized as citizens, they had no choice but to pay taxes. (Corning Museum.)

黄德純 (Wong Foey) was a champion of the people living in Tehama County. Referred to as the "Mayor of Chinatown," his efforts would delay the precipitous decline of Chinese American residents from leaving Tehama County for at least two generations. Wong Foey moved to America in 1862 and settled in Red Bluff in approximately 1876. (Tehama County Museum.)

Wong Foey was an equal opportunist, hiring white pickers for $1.25 per day in 1894 on the Cone ranch, pictured here. By 1900, Wong Foey hired Japanese pickers. Since Wong could speak and write English, he used his skills to negotiate labor contracts and started numerous Chinese business endeavors, including helping many throughout Tehama County to start their own Chinese businesses.

Wong Foey purchased this property pictured despite the Chinese Exclusion Act of 1882 and California enacting the Alien Land Law on May 3, 1913, barring Asian immigrants from owning land. Wong managed to maintain his ownership. Referred to as the Tang Foey residence is Gene Hing (right) who is the grandson of Charlie Ramsey standing next to Johnny On (left). It was located at 859 High (Rio) Street, Red Bluff, California.

In the background is a 684-square-foot Chinese Masonic Hall located at 824 High Street in Red Bluff, California, built in December 1904 by T.K. Johnson. The first floor had a large altar with elaborate finishes. The second floor was the lodge area for Mason members. The Chinese Masonic replaced the 洪顺堂 (Hong Shun Tang), which had 100 members by 1895 and was a branch of the first Hongmen society in San Francisco.

As early as 1893, Dr. Bo Do Hong created an annual tradition of a Chinese American banquet in Red Bluff. In 1908, the Bo Do Hong Company held the banquet at the Chinese Masonic Hall with 40 of the most prominent townsmen attending, merging the two cultures for the end of the Gregorian New Year. The event grew to 70 people by 1914. (Library of Congress.)

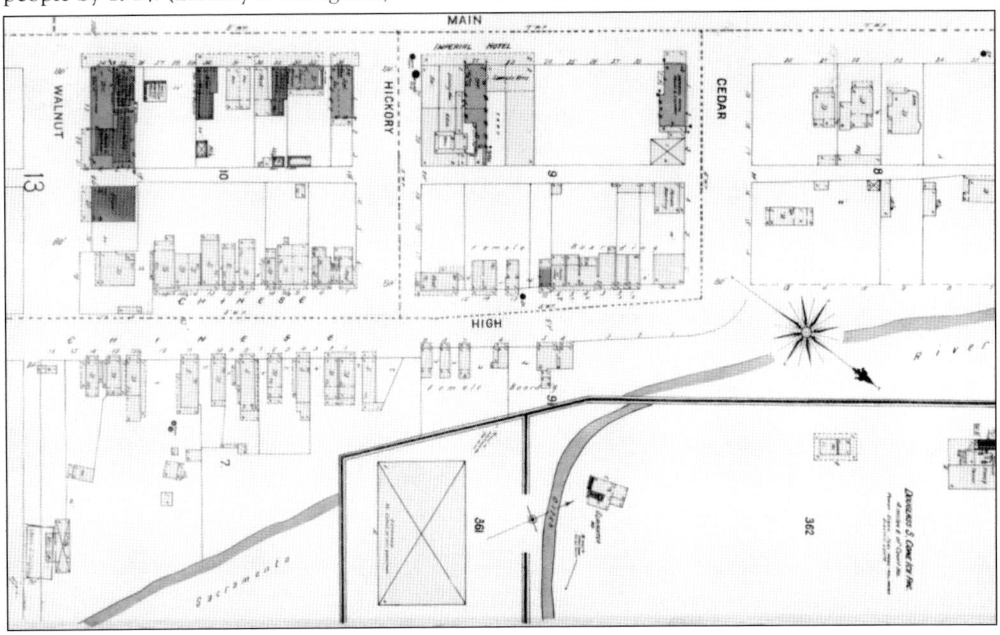

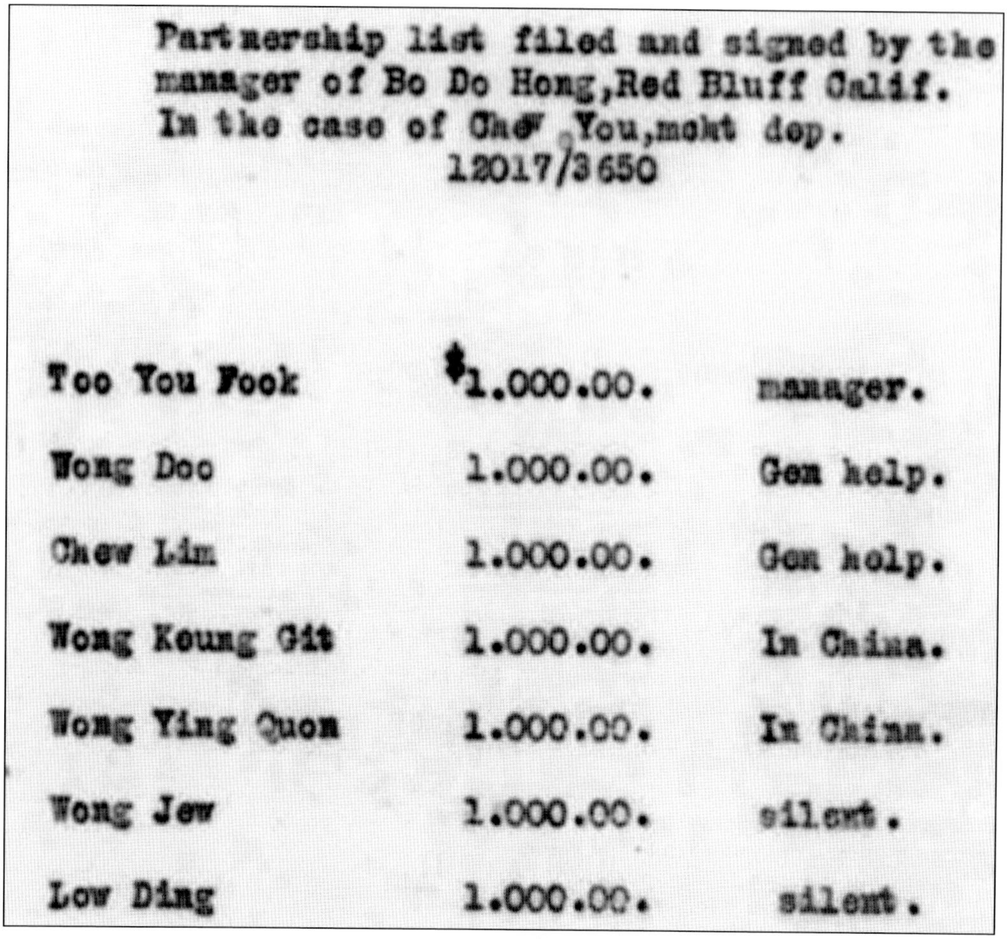

Partnership list filed and signed by the
manager of Bo Do Hong, Red Bluff Calif.
In the case of Chew You, mcht dep.
12017/3650

Too You Fook	$1.000.00.	manager.
Wong Doo	1.000.00.	Gen help.
Chew Lim	1.000.00.	Gen help.
Wong Koung Git	1.000.00.	In China.
Wong Ying Quon	1.000.00.	In China.
Wong Jew	1.000.00.	silent.
Low Ding	1.000.00.	silent.

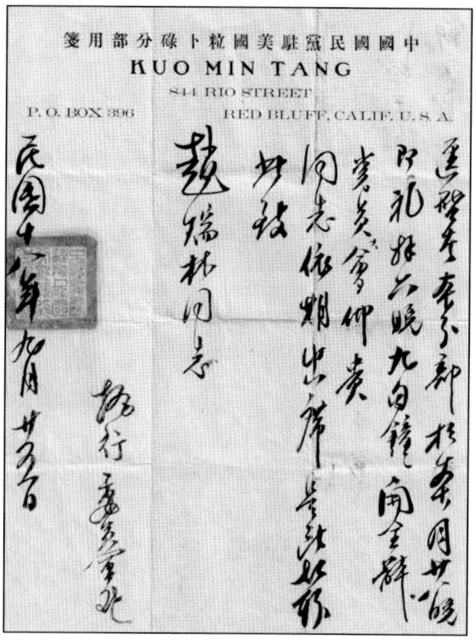

中國國民黨駐美國粒卜碌分部用箋
KUO MIN TANG
844 RIO STREET
P. O. BOX 396
RED BLUFF, CALIF. U. S. A.

Initially, the Chinese American banquets were just a few American friends and family, but as Bo Do Hong's friendships and his business grew, it became quite the annual attraction. He would decorate the banquet hall and begin festivities with him greeting and bidding guests farewell at the door. The event had grown so large that J.A. Owens and W.A. Fish aided in coordinating the annual festivity.

As China's political shifts changed in 1912, the Kuomintang was established at 844 High (Rio) Street and was connected to the Chew residence by a passageway. By 1927, the rise of the Kuomintang (Nationalist Party of China) changed many things. One could not afford to return to China, much less take the risk of being unable to return to America, with the ongoing war on the mainland.

Julia Chew is pictured in front of her birthplace on the right, the Bo Do Hong Company located at 838 High Street, Red Bluff, California, around 1923. The left building pictured is the Kuomintang, located at 844 High Street. Both the Kuomintang and the Bo Do Hong Company were the last of three wooden structures demolished in 1948.

This photograph was used in a newspaper to advertise the Bo Do Hong Company to a Caucasian audience. Dr. Bo Do Hong first arrived in 1865 as an educated doctor and established a Traditional Chinese Medicine practice by the 1870s census in Red Bluff. He was born in 1837. He was called by the name of the herbal practice, which means "Hall of the Protector of Health." (Courtesy of Wei-ling [Yuen] Louie.)

One could go into the Bo Do Hong Company and purchase herbs for his immediate ailment, buy a week's groceries, send money to the old country, play a few games of pai gow, and even get drunk on ng gah pei, provided he would not become a public nuisance. Shown is a banking bag from the Bo Do Hong Company, where the financial accounting was managed by Chew You.

During the 1880s, there were approximately 2,000 Chinese residents living in Red Bluff's Chinatown. This is the interior of the Bo Do Hong Company. Most goods were shipped from China by steamboat in cargo. The rear of the Bo Do Hong Company had a huge kitchen overlooking the Sacramento River with gigantic iron skillets to make meals. By 1910, both of Bo Do Hong's children, Keet Bo Do Hong and Tang Bo Do Hong, had died.

Chew You (Chew Suey Lum or Chew Siu Lim) was the accountant for the 1894 Dun Sow Hong Company, located at 306 Marchessault Street, Los Angeles; the Kwong Cheung Youn Company, located at 906 Dupont Street, San Francisco; and the Bo Do Hong Company. Pictured from left to right are Dick Chew, Chew You, Nettie (Chew) Ong, Chin See, Joe Chew, Julia Chew, Mrs. Ng Shee Chew holding Edward Chew, Violet (Chew) Dong, and Ned Chew.

After Dr. Bo Do Hong arranged the marriage of Dr. Chew Yuen to Mrs. Wong Shee, she settled in Red Bluff. She arrived in America in 1899. On paper, her father operated the herbal practice 福生堂 藥材 (Fook Sang Tong & Company), located at 744 Sacramento Street, San Francisco, California, near the Chew family's herbal practice, located on 906 Dupont Street, San Francisco, California. (Wei-ling [Yuen] Louie.)

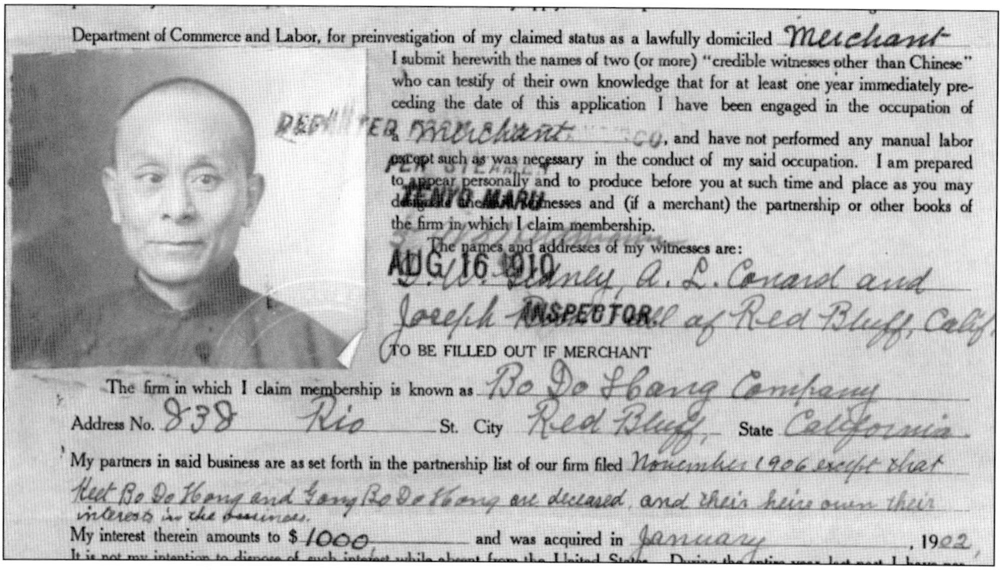

Department of Commerce and Labor, for preinvestigation of my claimed status as a lawfully domiciled Merchant
I submit herewith the names of two (or more) "credible witnesses other than Chinese" who can testify of their own knowledge that for at least one year immediately preceding the date of this application I have been engaged in the occupation of a Merchant ... Co, and have not performed any manual labor except such as was necessary in the conduct of my said occupation. I am prepared to appear personally and to produce before you at such time and place as you may designate the witnesses and (if a merchant) the partnership or other books of the firm in which I claim membership.
The names and addresses of my witnesses are:
D. W. ...nly, A. L. Conard and Joseph ... all of Red Bluff, Calif

AUG 16 1910
INSPECTOR

TO BE FILLED OUT IF MERCHANT
The firm in which I claim membership is known as Bo Do Hong Company
Address No. 838 Rio St. City Red Bluff, State California
My partners in said business are as set forth in the partnership list of our firm filed November 1906 except that Hut Bo Do Hong and Gong Bo Do Hong are deceased, and their heirs own their interests in the business.
My interest therein amounts to $ 1000 and was acquired in January, 1902

In 1903, Wong Toy (Toy Bo Do Hong or Wong Ying Gon), born in 1861, became a partner at the Bo Do Hong Company. He was previously a merchant for the Toy Kee Company located at 222 D Street, Portland, Oregon, and Lai Wah Yuen Company in Hong Kong. His wife was Fong Shee, and his children were Wong Lung Do (Foo Joe Yin), Wong Lung Seung, Wong Lung How, and Wong Ah Loy.

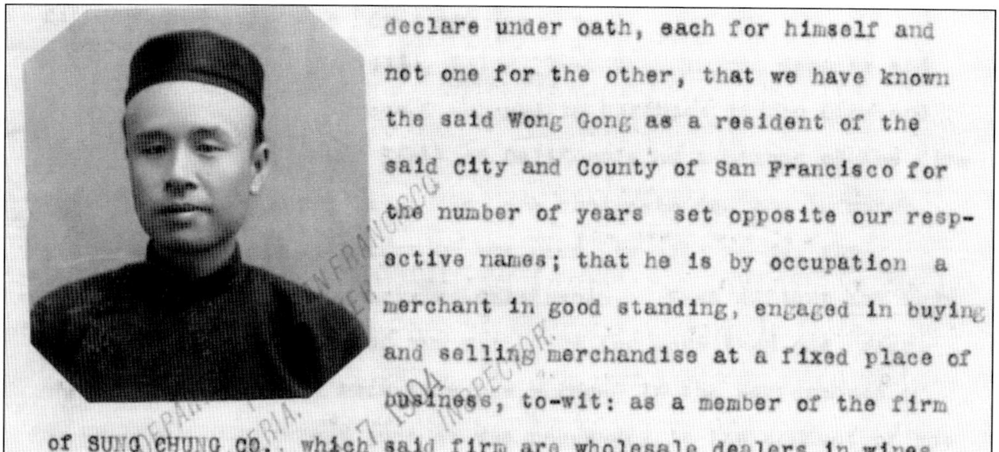

declare under oath, each for himself and not one for the other, that we have known the said Wong Gong as a resident of the said City and County of San Francisco for the number of years set opposite our respective names; that he is by occupation a merchant in good standing, engaged in buying and selling merchandise at a fixed place of business, to-wit: as a member of the firm of SUNG CHUNG CO., which said firm are wholesale dealers in wines and liquors; doing business at No. 605 Jackson street in the said

SIBERIA. OCT 7 1904 INSPECTOR

After the 1906 earthquake in San Francisco, Wong Gong invested in the Jok Kee general store, located at 724 High Street in Red Bluff, California. His children were Wong Poo (1889), Wong Hoy (1892), and Wong Lip (1904). In 1901, Wong Gong had a wholesale wine and liquor business called Sung Chung (Shung Coon) Company, located in San Francisco, California, at 605 Jackson Street, which eventually moved to 2602 Geary Street before settling in Red Bluff.

The Jok Kee Company, located second from the left, was operated by Wong Gong (manager), Wong Hoy (general help), Wong Jok (bookkeeper), and Leong Sing. The neighboring building was a restaurant located at 870 High Street and had a three-foot adjoining hallway in the rear where the kitchen was located. The store sold American goods from W.H. Fisher's grocery store on Main Street.

Department of Commerce and Labor for preinvestigation of my claimed status as a lawfully domiciled Merchant

I submit herewith the names of two (or more) "credible witnesses other than Chinese" who can testify of their own knowledge that for at least one year immediately preceding the date of this application I have been engaged in the occupation of a Merchant, and have not performed any manual labor except such as was necessary in the conduct of my said occupation. I am prepared to appear personally and to produce before you at such time and place as you may designate the said witnesses and (if a merchant) the partnership or other books of the firm in which I claim membership.

The names and addresses of my witnesses are:

A L Conard Red Bluff California

Fred Parks Red Bluff California

TO BE FILLED OUT IF MERCHANT

The firm in which I claim membership is known as Tai Wo Company

Address No. 812 High St. City Red Bluff State California

Despite the Chinese Exclusion Act and the McCreary Amendment in 1893, Wong never registered for a Certificate of Residence because of his merchant status. Wong Quong Yo (Wong Gong Hong) was a partner of the Tai Wo Company general store located at 812 High Street in Red Bluff. To perpetuate the criminalization of the Chinese community, this site was raided on June 29, 1911, for opium, but nothing was found.

Frank Hendricks was hired to oversee the ground-up construction of this two-story building located at 202-204 Walnut Street, Red Bluff, California. The O'Connor Brothers were hired to construct a banquet hall in the basement. In 2024, Joe Chew's granddaughter sought to purchase the building at the asking price to preserve it, but it was sold to the Resource Conservation District of Tehama County and converted into office use. (Wei-ling [Yuen] Louie.)

In 1899, Bo Do Hong sent for Chew Yuen (Too You Fook or Too Den Yen) to help with the practice. Pictured is the interior of 202-204 Walnut Street. Following the death of Bo Do Hong in 1909, Chew Yuen decided in 1915 that he would become a sole proprietor and buy out his fellow investors, renaming the business from Bo Do Hong Company to the Chew Yuen Company. Pictured from left to right are Robert Chew, Lew Ing Jung, and Letitia Frances Bo Do Hong Po-Wen Huang (Frances Too or Too Ngoot). (Wei-ling [Yuen] Louie.)

Pictured is the living room of Dr. Chew Yuen, who eventually became one of the town's leading citizens. On the right is Robert Chew Yuen (Robert Bo Do Hong or Too Suey Wee). Dr. Chew Yuen would be arrested several times for practicing Traditional Chinese Medicine, and W.A. Fish successfully defended him. Below this room is where the eagerly attended Chinese American banquets were held. (Wei-ling [Yuen] Louie.)

Chew Yuen Company had several medicinal plants. From left to right are Letitia Frances Bo Do Hong Po-Wen Huang (Frances Too or Too Ngoot), Robert Chew Yuen (Robert Bo Do Hong or Too Suey Wee), Wong Shee Lee holding Chew Owen Yuen (Too Chew Owen or Too Thin Wee), Too See Ying (Harry Too), Dr. Chew Yuen, and Margaret Rose Bo Do Hong (Too Gim). (Wei-ling [Yuen] Louie.)

Logging had become a significant part of Tehama County's economic development since it was the easiest method for addressing rapid population growth and could quickly build cabins, stores, saloons, and even heat the buildings; hence, massive job growth in the lumber industry was required to respond to the demand. This image is of Jackson and Hickory Streets outside the Red Bluff Railroad Park, where carloads of logs filled the trains.

In this c. 1920s image, from left to right are Too See Ying, Ned Chew, and Dick Chew, pictured inside the Railroad Park on Walnut Street and Madison Street in Red Bluff, California. In 1872, the Central Pacific Railroad to Red Bluff was completed. This was the end of a great "river" highway to the gold fields. The railroad tracks were adjacent to the Sierra Lumber Company.

In 1904, the Home Restaurant was purchased by Yee Sam Yuen from C.S. Slater. The restaurant did well because it was strategically located across from the Railroad Depot at 619 Walnut Street, Red Bluff, California. Pictured are Won Chew, Chew Owen Yuen, Violet (Chew) Dong, and Mrs. Ng Shee Chew with newborn Nettie (Chew) Ong.

In 1903, Chew You joined his family, Dr. Bo Do Hong and Dr. Chew Yuen, in Red Bluff. Since he had been a cook in Pasadena, his second job was cooking for Yee Sam Yuen at the Home Restaurant before buying it with Dr. Chew Yuen in 1916. Pictured is an elder, Dick Chew, and Won Chew in front of the California Café (previously the Home Restaurant).

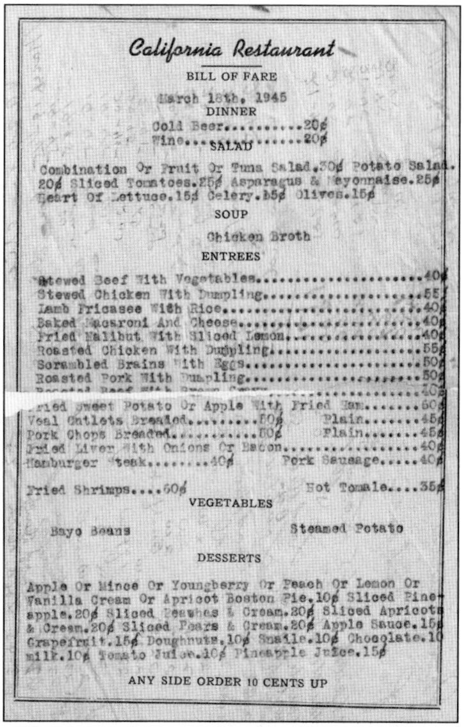

California Restaurant

BILL OF FARE

March 18th, 1945

DINNER

Cold Beer..........20¢
Wine...............20¢

SALAD

Combination Or Fruit Or Tuna Salad.30¢ Potato Salad.
20¢ Sliced Tomatoes.25¢ Asparagus & Mayonnaise.25¢
Heart Of Lettuce.15¢ Celery.15¢ Olives.15¢

SOUP

Chicken Broth

ENTREES

Stewed Beef With Vegetables.....................40¢
Stewed Chicken With Dumpling....................55¢
Lamb Fricasee With Rice.........................40¢
Baked Macaroni And Cheese.......................40¢
Fried Halibut With Sliced Lemon.................40¢
Roasted Chicken With Dumpling...................55¢
Scrambled Brains With Eggs......................50¢
Roasted Pork With Dumpling......................50¢
[illegible]....40¢
Fried Sweet Potato Or Apple With Fried Ham.......60¢
Veal Cutlets Breaded.........50¢ Plain.......45¢
Pork Chops Breaded...........50¢ Plain.......45¢
Fried Liver With Onions Or Bacon................40¢
Hamburger Steak........40¢ Pork Sausage.....40¢

Fried Shrimps....60¢ Hot Tomale....35¢

VEGETABLES

Bayo Beans Steamed Potato

DESSERTS

Apple Or Mince Or Youngberry Or Peach Or Lemon Or
Vanilla Cream Or Apricot Boston Pie.10¢ Sliced Pine-
apple.20¢ Sliced Peaches & Cream.20¢ Sliced Apricots
& Cream.20¢ Sliced Pears & Cream.20¢ Apple Sauce.15¢
Grapefruit.15¢ Doughnuts.10¢ Snails.10¢ Chocolate.10
milk.10¢ Tomato Juice.10¢ Pineapple Juice.15¢

ANY SIDE ORDER 10 CENTS UP

Chew You and son Dick Chew eventually fully transferred the ownership of the California Café from Dr. Chew Yuen. Shown here is the menu of their American cuisine, which differs substantially from Chinese American food as we know it today.

Pictured is head chef Dick Chew cooking in the kitchen with his sister Nettie (Chew) Ong at the California Café. Dick was sensitive to the needy. During the Great Depression, Dick did not have the heart to turn anyone away hungry. He kept a cigar box filled with the names of those who had eaten a meal on an honor system. Some paid their debt, but many probably did not.

It is not known exactly when Yee Kim Sing opened his first restaurant, but one of the earliest records places him in Los Molinos, California, where his restaurant Kim Sing tragically burned down in 1915. Pictured from left to right are (first row) Bonnie Lim, Jeannie Lim, and Ronnie Lim; (second row) Kim Sing, Peter Lim, and Mei Si (May) Lim. Kim Sing lived at many places, including residing at the former Chinese temple located at 774 High Street, Red Bluff. (Jeannie May Lim.)

Kim Sing immigrated in 1878 from 宏村 (Hongcun Village) at the age of 14, becoming a 19th-century restaurateur, operating Kim Sing in Los Molinos (1900s), Thuresson's Restaurant in Red Bluff (1913), Orpheum Grill in Redding (1928), Roosevelt Café in Red Bluff (1934), Kim Sing Chop Suey (1939, pictured) and Lim's Chop Suey (1950), both in Redding. (Jeannie May Lim.)

Kim Sing's restaurant legacy would be continued by his adopted son, Peter Lim, and his granddaughters for over 107 consecutive years. It originally opened as the House of Lim's in Redding, and later Peter renamed it to Lim's Café. It became one of the last 19th-century generational family-operated Chinese American restaurants in all of Northern California, closing September 6, 2022. (Jeannie May Lim.)

Peter Lim (Lim Shew Sui or Lim Tung Wah) had immigrated to America in 1924, living at 823 High Street in Red Bluff with Yee Ong and Chung Yee. All worked at the Tremont Hotel, with Peter and Ong as waiters and Chung Yee as a chef. From left to right are (first row) unidentified and Peter Lim; (second row) Margaret Rose Bo Do Hong, Violet (Chew) Dong, and Nettie (Chew) Ong. (Wei-ling [Yuen] Louie.)

Pictured from left to right are Too See Ying, Dick Chew, and Ned Chew dressed in their Sunday best at the Methodist church in Red Bluff. Dick's father, Chew You, immigrated to the United States as a Methodist missionary. The Chew family remained loyal to the Christian faith, attending the Methodist Church and Epworth League.

Too See Way (Peter A. Chan or Too Pei Chan), born in 1891 in China, was required to immigrate in 1909 by his father, Dr. Chew Yuen. He became the last to operate the Foo & Wing Herb Company located at 564 Massachusetts Avenue in Boston, Massachusetts. In 1923, he married widower Ho Yee Chan, previously married to Dr. Tom Wing (Tom Duck Sam), relative of the great Dr. Li Po Tai.

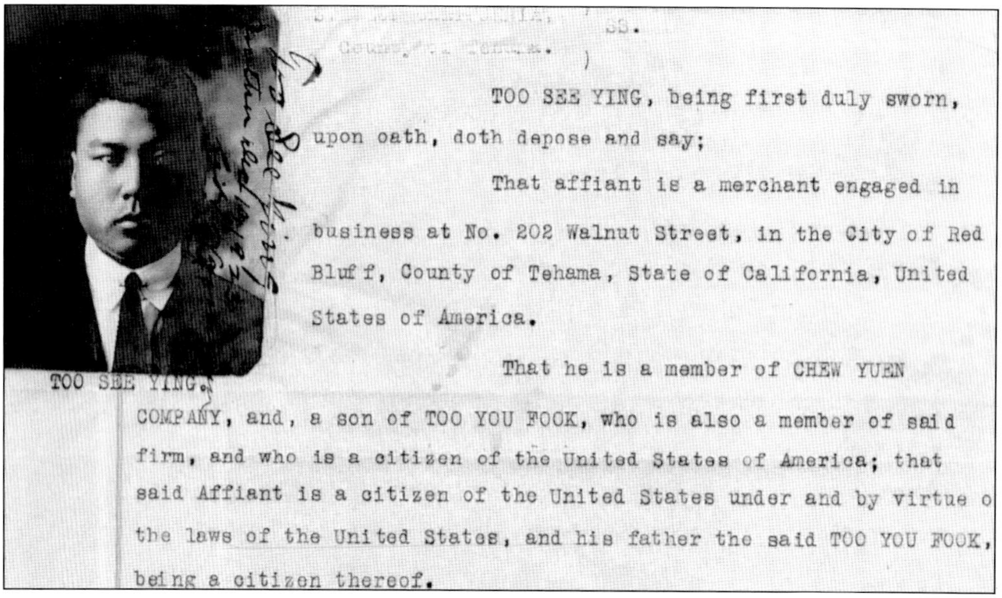

SS.

TOO SEE YING, being first duly sworn, upon oath, doth depose and say;

That affiant is a merchant engaged in business at No. 202 Walnut Street, in the City of Red Bluff, County of Tehama, State of California, United States of America.

TOO SEE YING.

That he is a member of CHEW YUEN COMPANY, and, a son of TOO YOU FOOK, who is also a member of said firm, and who is a citizen of the United States of America; that said Affiant is a citizen of the United States under and by virtue o the laws of the United States, and his father the said TOO YOU FOOK, being a citizen thereof.

Pictured in 1913 is Too See Ying (Harry Too). Born on December 16, 1894, in China, he briefly worked for his father, Dr. Chew Yuen, in Red Bluff. However, he went against the family tradition of becoming a Traditional Chinese Medicine physician by opening Harry's Laundry in Brooklyn, New York, which is still a laundry business in 2024. He had nine children with Chin Lin Hai.

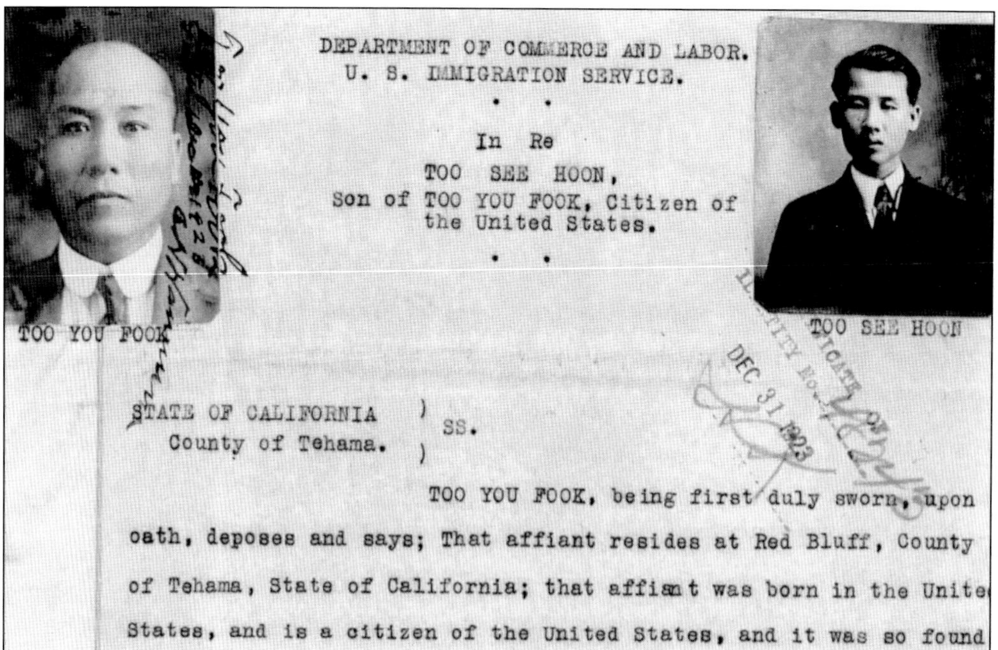

DEPARTMENT OF COMMERCE AND LABOR.
U. S. IMMIGRATION SERVICE.

In Re
TOO SEE HOON,
Son of TOO YOU FOOK, Citizen of
the United States.

TOO YOU FOOK

TOO SEE HOON

DEC 31 1923

STATE OF CALIFORNIA) SS.
County of Tehama.)

TOO YOU FOOK, being first duly sworn, upon oath, deposes and says; That affiant resides at Red Bluff, County of Tehama, State of California; that affiant was born in the Unite States, and is a citizen of the United States, and it was so found

Too See Hoon (Too See Hung) is pictured with his father, Dr. Chew Yuen, where he worked briefly as a bookkeeper. He immigrated in 1922 with the help of J.A. Owen's persistent advocacy to release him from Angel Island. He had three sons with Chew Shee.

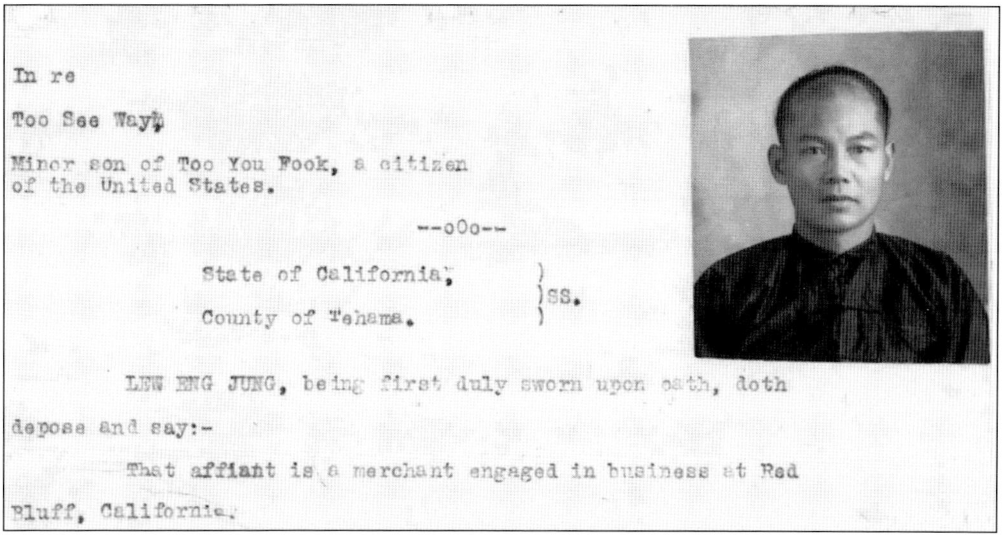

In re

Too See Way

Minor son of Too You Fook, a citizen
of the United States.

--oOo--

State of California,)
)SS.
County of Tehama.)

LEW ENG JUNG, being first duly sworn upon oath, doth depose and say:-

That affiant is a merchant engaged in business at Red Bluff, California.

Forced to evacuate by firemen in 1929, Lew Ing Jung tried to save the Chinese Masonic Hall after the electrical wiring next door caught on fire. 刘英榮 (Lew Ing Jung) was born in 1865 and married Mrs. Lew Shee, born in 1867. Their children were Lew Quon On (Frank On or Lew Qwon On), born 1892, Lew Den Soo, born 1897, and Lew Keun Sen, born 1905.

After Lew Ing Jung emigrated from China to America, he worked at the Bo Do Hong Company and eventually retired from the Chew Yuen Company. Pictured in his later years as the caretaker for the Chew children. From left to right are Ned Chew, Dick Chew, Lew Ing Jung with Violet (Chew) Dong, and Too See Ying.

The American Café, located at 518 Walnut Street in Red Bluff, was owned by the former head chef Henry Yuen, Jimmie Yuen, and Lee Toy from 1918 until 1920. It was sold after the partners accused Henry of embezzlement. Henry sold the restaurant to L.C. Nickerson in 1927. He purchased the State Grill on Main Street and the Golden Eagle Café until 1918, when he sold it to Wong Bing. (*Red Bluff Daily News.*)

In 1928, Lew Quon On (Frank On), pictured on the right, bought out Henry Yuen's lease for the American Café located at 516 Walnut Street in Red Bluff, becoming well known for Mexican tamales. He was born in 1892 in 银屏镇 (Yin Ping), Anhui Province, China. Frank married the daughter of Mr. Lung Jung Lee and Mrs. Lung See.

陳孔祝 (Wing Jung Chin) is pictured visiting his sister Mrs. Chin See in Red Bluff's Chinatown around 1925. From left to right are (first row) Nettie (Chew) Ong, Joe You Chew, and baby Julia Chew; (second row) Chew You, Mrs. Ng Shee, Mrs. Chin See, and Violet Chew (Dong); (third row) Dick Chew and Wing Jung Chin.

In 1920, 陳孔祝 Wing Jung Chin, born in 1899, immigrated to America as a paper son. He owned a laundry at 147 East Merrimack Street in Lowell, Massachusetts. His son 陳想華 (Henry Chin or Chin Theung Wah) immigrated in 1931, while his wife, Lu Gam Fhoung, immigrated in 1948. Wing frequently visited his sister Chin See in Red Bluff, where his son later settled. (Chin family.)

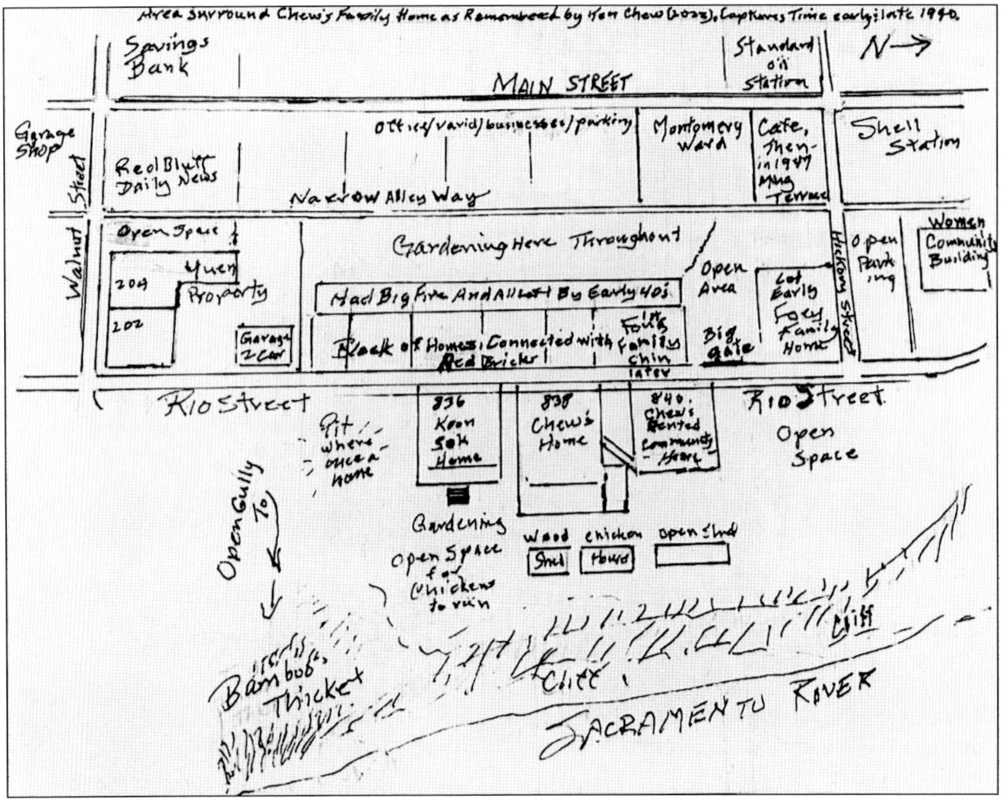

After a major fire in 1908, landlord Mrs. Hearns commissioned the construction of a new brick building with a basement. It was home to the Fong family while they worked for Arthur L. Conrad, who provided housing as part of their employment agreement. In recent years, this location has become plagued with tunnel folklore. This drawing is by Dr. Kenneth Kendall Chew.

In this image, taken in Red Bluff, pictured from left to right are Lee Mee Gum with son Arthur Fong, husband Jimmy Gum You Fong, and son Edward Fong. Their sons were among the few Chinese Americans born at the hospital, with youngest son Robert contributing to this book. (Robert Fong.)

Eddie Kontoon Fong, born on March 16, 1905, worked as a cook at the Tremont Hotel. He married Ruby Gee Fong (Sue Gee Fong) of New Orleans, Louisiana. All of their children, with the exception of Ronald, were born at 844 High Street, Red Bluff: Edward "Eddie" Jr., born 1932; George, born 1934; David, born 1937; and Harry, born 1939. Eddie died in Sacramento on September 17, 1991.

After the Conard family sold the Tremont Hotel to the Forward family in October 1945, the restaurant changed from American cuisine to French, thus leaving many in the Chinese community unemployed and forcing the Fong family to relocate to Colusa, followed by Tenth and W Street in Sacramento, California.

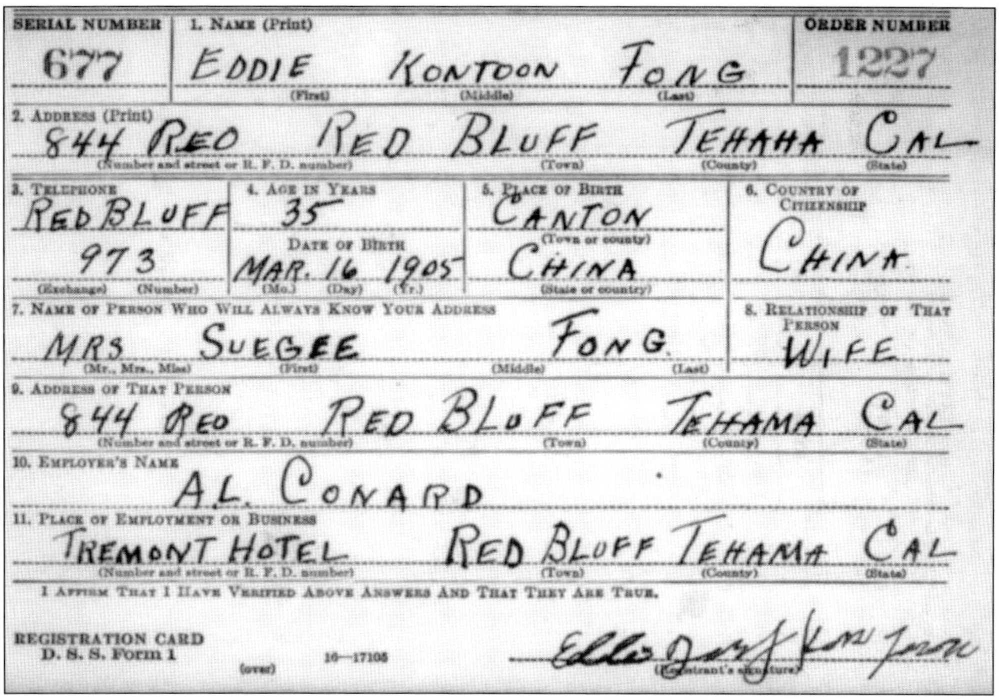

SERIAL NUMBER 677

1. NAME (Print) EDDIE (First) KONTOON (Middle) FONG (Last)

ORDER NUMBER 1227

2. ADDRESS (Print) 844 REO (Number and street or R. F. D. number) RED BLUFF (Town) TEHAHA (County) CAL (State)

3. TELEPHONE RED BLUFF (Exchange) 973 (Number)

4. AGE IN YEARS 35

DATE OF BIRTH MAR. (Mo.) 16 (Day) 1905 (Yr.)

5. PLACE OF BIRTH CANTON (Town or county) CHINA (State or country)

6. COUNTRY OF CITIZENSHIP CHINA

7. NAME OF PERSON WHO WILL ALWAYS KNOW YOUR ADDRESS MRS (Mr., Mrs., Miss) SUEGEE (First) (Middle) FONG (Last)

8. RELATIONSHIP OF THAT PERSON WIFE

9. ADDRESS OF THAT PERSON 844 REO (Number and street or R. F. D. number) RED BLUFF (Town) TEHAMA (County) CAL (State)

10. EMPLOYER'S NAME AL. CONARD

11. PLACE OF EMPLOYMENT OR BUSINESS TREMONT HOTEL (Number and street or R. F. D. number) RED BLUFF (Town) TEHAMA (County) CAL (State)

I AFFIRM THAT I HAVE VERIFIED ABOVE ANSWERS AND THAT THEY ARE TRUE.

REGISTRATION CARD
D. S. S. Form 1 (over) 16—17105

Eddie Fong Kontoon (Registrant's signature)

Fong Kee You lived at 825 High Street, Red Bluff, which today is named Historic Chinatown Alley. He was born in Sacramento on August 26, 1881, and worked at the Blue Ribbon Café in Red Bluff. His son Mee Ning Fong (Fong Ming Ning), born January 1, 1922, worked for Arthur L. Conard as a cook, and later lived at 1102 Solano Street in Corning, California, in 1940. (NARA.)

Extended relatives such as Joe How and his family visited Red Bluff. The 陳 (How) family lived on Grant Avenue in San Francisco. From left to right are (first row) James Chew, Arthur How, Chris Chew, Mrs. Ng Shee, Dr. Kenneth Chew, and Lorena How; (second row) Patrick How, Jane (Chew) Jung, John S. How, Dick Chew with wife Chin See, grand aunt, Betty (How) Tung, and Nettie (Chew) Ong.

The Historic Loomis Museum was another enjoyable site to visit. It was built in 1927 at Lassen Volcanic National Park in California. Pictured enjoying the museum are two unidentified elders, Letitia Frances Po-Wen Huang (Bo Do Hong), two unidentified elders, Helen Yuen on the steps, and Margaret Rose Bo Do Hong by the tree. (Wei-ling [Yuen] Louie.)

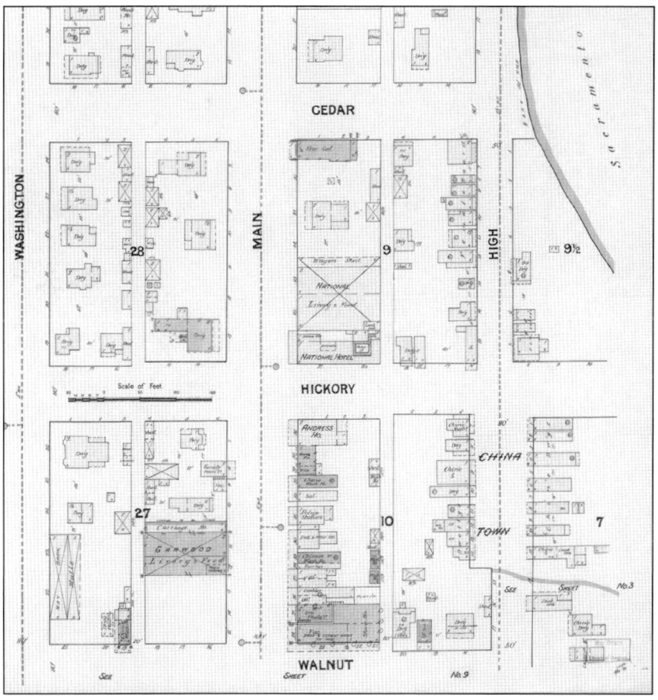

For many years, there was the Quong Lee store located in Tehama, California, which served as a general store selling household items such as food, groceries, and apparel. Restocking required Mr. Lee to return to China from Red Bluff. (Library of Congress.)

Well known as Big Boss Sam (or China Sam) and Jew Sing, these two men oversaw hiring for the peach, nectarine, and apricot orchards in Deer Creek. This 1939 photograph captures them standing in front of their cabin, which once stood northwest of the Deer Creek Bridge. (TCGHS.)

Known as Charlie "Peanut," he lived in Vina before moving to Tehama, where he worked as a garden foreman for Sam Lee. A beloved member of the community for over 60 years, he died at 79 in a tragic railroad accident and rests in an unmarked grave in Tehama Cemetery.

Hong Fook Tung, pictured in 1912 with his wife, Susie, was known for most of his life as "Sam Lee," born in 1867 in Oroville, California. He and his parents briefly lived in China. He returned in 1887 to Oroville, followed by Tehama. Every year for Sam's birthday and Chinese New Year, he would invite the entire town to celebrate with him. (Tehama County Museum.)

In the photograph at the top, Sam Lee is wearing traditional Chinese silk shoes, and in this picture, he wears American-style shoes, bending them back, making them slippers. The entire town of Tehama had a farewell celebration for Sam when he decided to briefly return to China before settling in Auburn, California, with his sister Lena Yue. His shoes can be visited at the Auburn Joss House Museum, operated by his great-nephew Dustin Yue. (Luther L. Clements.)

Tehama County's first rodeo was held in 1918 at A.H. Clough Ranch, Los Molinos, and later moved to Red Bluff. It was an annual event that brought business to Chinese restaurants like the Ming Terrace but was marred by unfriendly cowboy patrons. Businesses would decorate for the festivities and stay open late. (Wei-ling [Yuen] Louie.)

Charlie Sun (left) worked in Lewiston and later as a vegetable delivery driver for Sam Lee in Tehama while residing in Los Molinos with his wife, Sally (right). Born June 16, 1876, Charlie was well-known by the Wong clan in Northern California for his work as a miner. He moved to Williams before settling in Stockton, where Charlie passed away on May 29, 1937. (Shelton Yip.)

Sally (left), pictured with her children, was especially gifted with growing flowers and maintained her entrepreneurial spirit after her husband, Charlie, passed away. She was born in 1883 in French Gulch, Shasta County. She died in 1954, and her siblings included Frank Wong, Dewey Wong, Wong Wing Suey (Wong Wing Non or Billy Wong), and Ed Wong. She settled at 546 East Church Street in Stockton, California. (Shelton Yip.)

Wong Hing Tang (Wong Chong Hing) first worked for the Kraft family, then as a farmer for John Moran in Corning. He emigrated as a student in 1900 from Shin Sin Village, Bok Bar, 新寧 (Sunning District), China. On July 30, 1907, he was denied entry into America due to trachoma and remained in China until April 22, 1908. He returned as a merchant of the Chew Yuen Company.

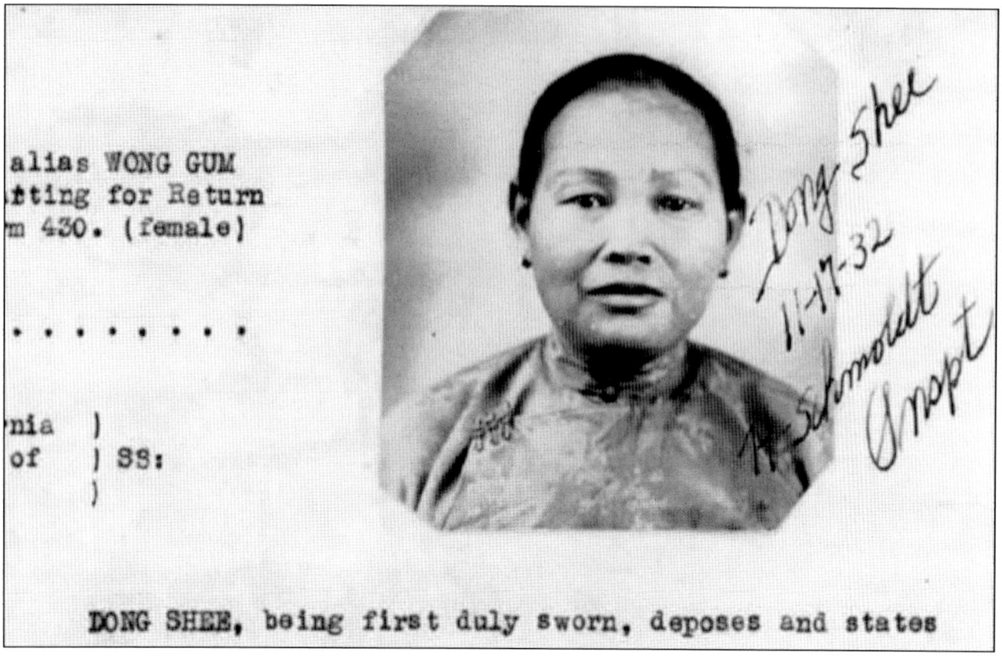

On April 21, 1932, the entire community of Corning held a heartfelt farewell celebration for the Wong family after Shee Hing (pictured) asked to return to China due to her dementia. Wong Hing married Dong Shee Hing (Dong Chun Hor) from Ng Hoy Village, Chew Ging, Sun Ning District, China, and was the daughter of Dong Jeung Cheung. She immigrated to Corning, California, on September 11, 1916.

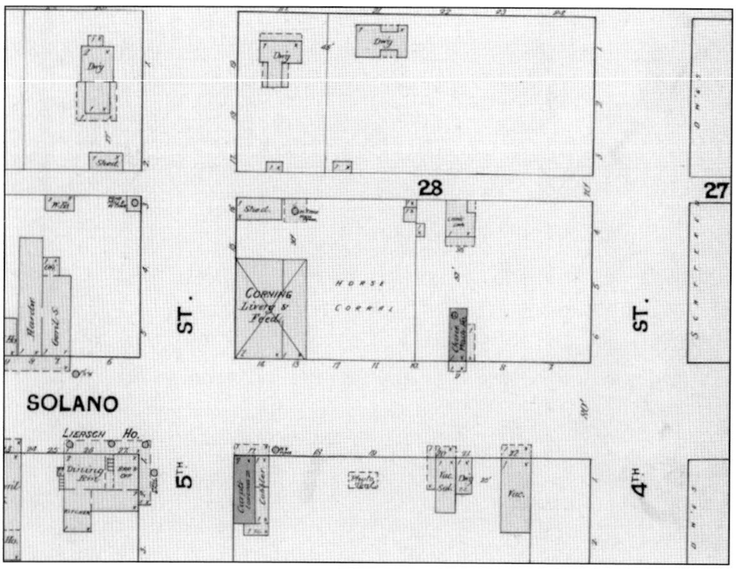

Over the years, owners such as Harry Merrigold and later W.N. Woodson of Hotel Maywood, located one block away from the railroad depot in Corning, California, employed many Chinese cooks. Some favorites included Harold Ho, the head chef, with Henry Fong as the meat cook, Kai Wong as the pantry man, and Sing Jew as a dishwasher. (Library of Congress.)

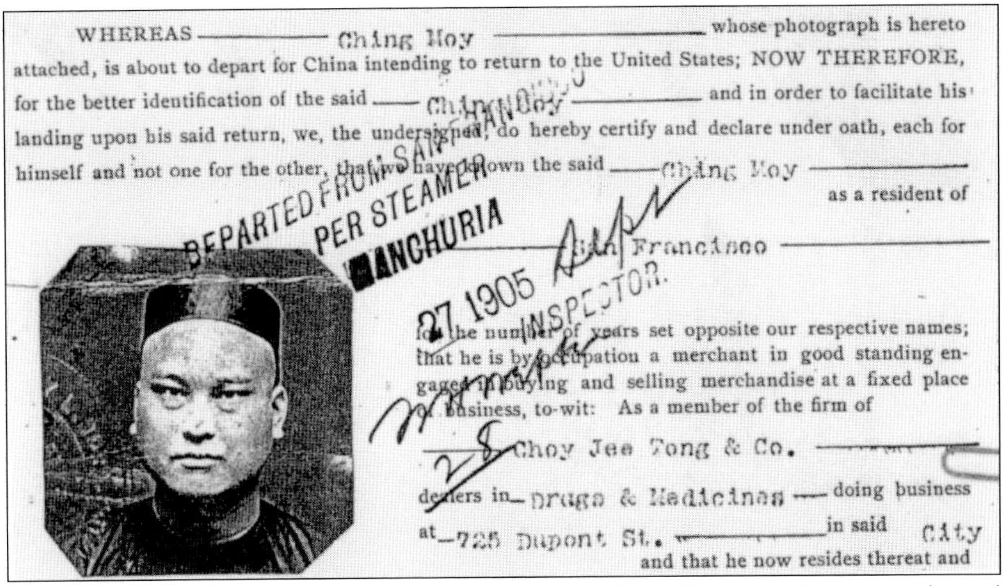

WHEREAS ——— Ching Moy ——— whose photograph is hereto attached, is about to depart for China intending to return to the United States; NOW THEREFORE, for the better identification of the said ——— Ching Moy ——— and in order to facilitate his landing upon his said return, we, the undersigned, do hereby certify and declare under oath, each for himself and not one for the other, that we have known the said ——— Ching Moy ——— as a resident of

——— San Francisco ———

for the number of years set opposite our respective names; that he is by occupation a merchant in good standing engaged in buying and selling merchandise at a fixed place of business, to-wit: As a member of the firm of

——— Choy Jee Tong & Co. ———

dealers in ——— Drugs & Medicines ——— doing business at ——— 725 Dupont St. ——— in said City and that he now resides thereat and

After the 1906 earthquake, Chin Moy relocated and started the Wah Kee and Company, located at 122 South Colusa Street in Willows, California. Like many businesses, the location was prone to fires. Chin Moy emigrated in 1888 as a partner of Choy Jee Tong Drug Company, located at 725 Dupont Street, in San Francisco. He died in May 1921 and is buried at the Go Mee Liang Hill ancestral hall.

Sadly, Chin Moy died when his son Albert Git Lee Chan was only six years old. Albert (left) is pictured with the owner of Mineral Lodge, Husky Beresford, and another colleague. Albert was born in China on June 15, 1915, but knew little about his father due to the Chinese Exclusion Act of 1882. (Janet Chan.)

Pictured is the Mineral Lodge in Mineral, California, before it burned down in 1949. The Beresford family favored hiring Chinese workers, mainly from the Yee and Chin clans. Most notable was Frank Toy, who was remembered for his love of Chinese games and traveling from Mineral to Susanville or Reno to gamble. (Janet Chan.)

This is the interior of the coffee shop located at Mineral Lodge, which employed people of various ethnicities but favored Chinese cooks to prepare American comfort food. Since it was a full-service restaurant, men working at the Mineral Mill ate here. Florence Ting SooHoo worked as a housekeeper, holding her daughter in the back left of this picture. (Janet Chan.)

Pictured is Albert Git Lee Chan's mother-in-law, Dr. Wong Kin Chin, with her four granddaughters. All were born in Red Bluff, California. Dr. Wong Kin Chin held a medical doctor degree in western medicine from Hackett Medical College for Women in Guangzhou, established in 1905 under the sponsorship of Protestant missionaries. By 1936, the medical center was known as Sun Yat-sen Medical College. She lived at 15 Han Kow Road, on the third floor, in Kowloon, Hong Kong, before settling in San Francisco. (Janet Chan.)

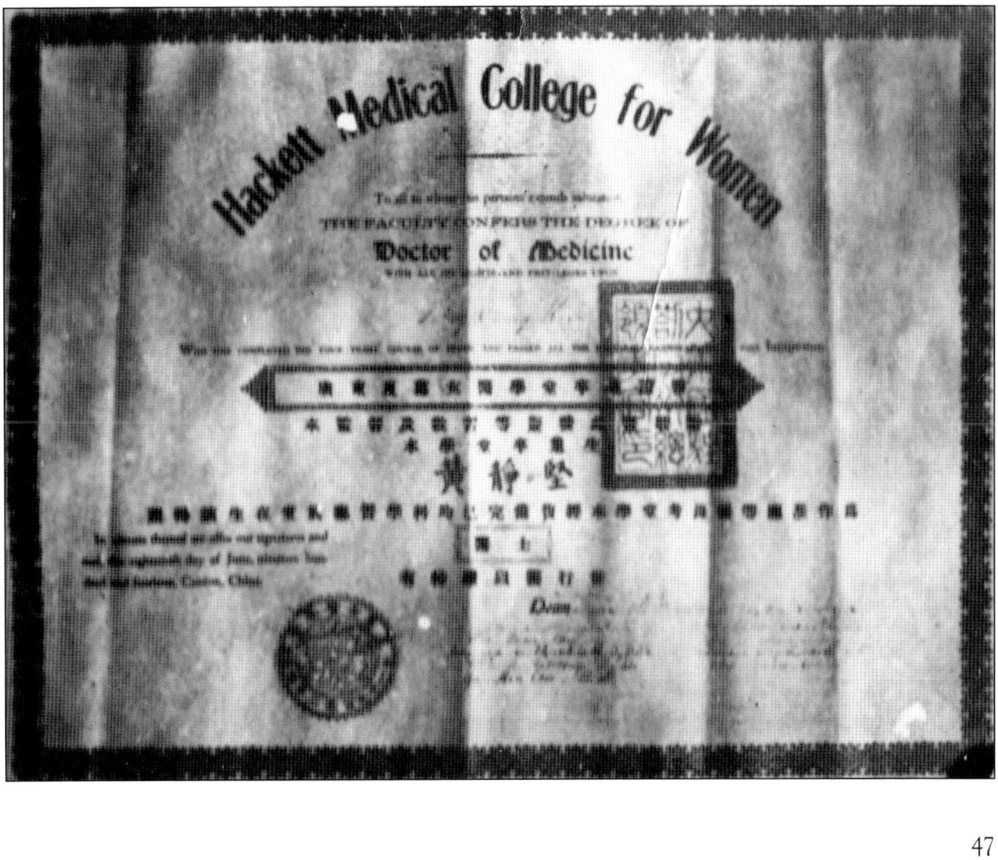

Mr. Lew Jung (Lie Jung, Hei Shoon, or Fong Shew Ming) was a cook for the Logan Brothers' cattle ranch. He purchased the Pearsons Ranch and, by 1932, purchased 137-139 North Butte Street, Willows, California, where he operated a highly successful Chinese bar-restaurant and rice farm. Lew was born in San Francisco on March 26, 1904, and is pictured with his wife. (Lew and Fong family.)

Dr. Kenneth Kendall Chew was born on October 29, 1933, at the Bo Do Hong Company to Dick Chew and Chin See. His eventful childhood hunting and fishing would propel his youthful aspirations, becoming a 20th-century pioneer known as the Oyster King, revolutionizing the science of aquaculture across the world today. From left to right are Edward Chew, Chris Chew, James Chew, and Dr. Kenneth Chew.

Two

Angel Island Immigration Process

After years of racial hostility and anti-immigration, in 1882, the Chinese Exclusion Act was passed by the 47th US Congress. The passage of the federal law would immediately impact Tehama County and its longtime Chinese residents, including prohibiting some American-born Chinese from becoming US citizens. In 1884, the courts ruled that Chinese wives of domiciled laborers were laborers by default of their husbands' status, further reducing their immigration. It was the first time a law was passed to exclude and prohibit a specific nationality. In 1892, the Geary Act expanded the law to require people of Chinese origin to carry an identification certificate or face deportation. The McCreary Act of 1893 made it more difficult for Chinese business owners to qualify for US entry by raising the burden of proof and broadening the grounds for exclusion by not only requiring witnesses to know the applicant for a minimum of one year but also further defining the exclusion of laborers as merchants, laundry owners, miners, and fishermen.

As part of the new immigration laws, the first detention was a shed known as a Chinese Jail located on the San Francisco wharf. The interior was 100 square feet with whitewashed windows and wire netting, squeezing up to 200 men without tables or chairs. Some hung themselves out of misery. Moreover, it was not uncommon for there to be several objections on the immigration papers. On January 21, 1910, steamship passengers were sent to the new detention center on Angel Island, known as the "Ellis Island of the West," with its main purpose of stopping Chinese immigration before entering the 富大金山(Gum Saan Dai Fow). For a person of Chinese origin or with the appearance of Asian ancestry, they were placed in barracks while their belongings were fumigated. They were checked for diseases through a culturally violating process, as well as subjected to harsh hau gong (interrogation) and lengthy incarceration. Angel Island was open until August 11, 1940.

Today, one can better understand immigration policies by reflecting upon the Angel Island experiences of Tehama County's Chinatown residents.

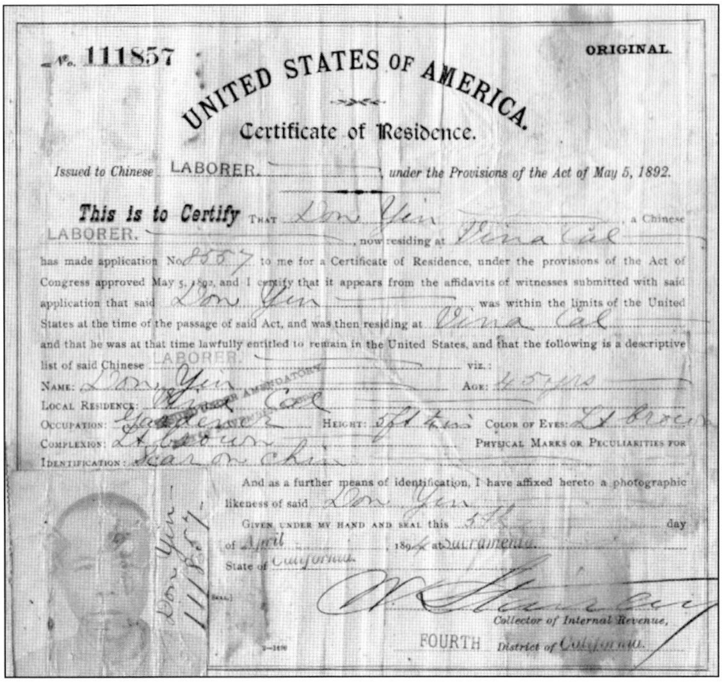

No. 111857 ORIGINAL.

UNITED STATES OF AMERICA.

Certificate of Residence.

Issued to Chinese LABORER, *under the Provisions of the Act of May 5, 1892.*

This is to Certify THAT Don Yin, a Chinese LABORER, now residing at Vina Cal has made application No. 8557 to me for a Certificate of Residence, under the provisions of the Act of Congress approved May 5, 1892, and I certify that it appears from the affidavits of witnesses submitted with said application that said Don Yin was within the limits of the United States at the time of the passage of said Act, and was then residing at Vina Cal and that he was at that time lawfully entitled to remain in the United States, and that the following is a descriptive list of said Chinese LABORER viz.:

NAME: Don Yin AGE: 45 yrs

LOCAL RESIDENCE: Vina Cal

OCCUPATION: Gardener HEIGHT: 5 ft 4 in COLOR OF EYES: Lt brown

COMPLEXION: Lt brown PHYSICAL MARKS OR PECULIARITIES FOR IDENTIFICATION: Scar on chin

And as a further means of identification, I have affixed hereto a photographic likeness of said Don Yin.

GIVEN UNDER MY HAND AND SEAL this 5th day of April, 1894 at Sacramento State of California

Collector of Internal Revenue, FOURTH District of California.

The Geary Act of 1892 required all Chinese residents in the United States to carry a resident permit, with failure to do so resulting in deportation or a year of hard labor. The McCreary Amendment of 1893 required, for the first time, that photographic identification be included on all registration certificates. Depicted is Don Yin in 1894, who was a 45-year-old gardener in Vina, California. (California Historical Society.)

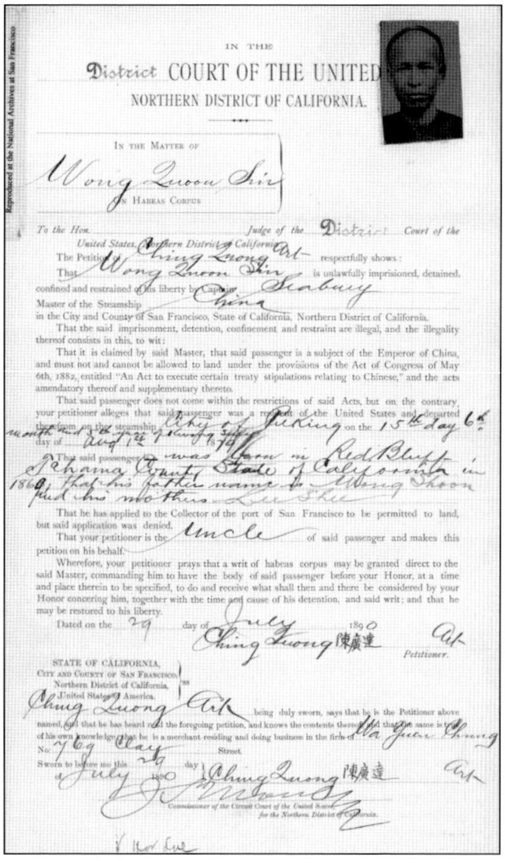

Reproduced at the National Archives at San Francisco

IN THE District COURT OF THE UNITED

NORTHERN DISTRICT OF CALIFORNIA.

IN THE MATTER OF Wong Quoon Sin ON HABEAS CORPUS

To the Hon. *Judge of the* District *Court of the United States, Northern District of California.*

The Petition of Ching Quong Ark respectfully shows:

That Wong Quoon Sin is unlawfully imprisoned, detained, confined and restrained of his liberty by Captain Seabury Master of the Steamship China in the City and County of San Francisco, State of California, Northern District of California.

That the said imprisonment, detention, confinement and restraint are illegal, and the illegality thereof consists in this, to wit:

That it is claimed by said Master, that said passenger is a subject of the Emperor of China, and must not and cannot be allowed to land under the provisions of the Act of Congress of May 6th, 1882, entitled "An Act to execute certain treaty stipulations relating to Chinese," and the acts amendatory thereof and supplementary thereto.

That said passenger does not come within the restrictions of said Acts, but on the contrary, your petitioner alleges that said passenger was a resident of the United States and departed therefrom on the steamship City of Peking on the 15th day 6th month and 5th year of Kwong Sui day of Aug 1st 1879

That said passenger was born in Red Bluff Tehama County State of California in 1869, that his father name is Wong Shoon and his mother Lee Shee

That he has applied to the Collector of the port of San Francisco to be permitted to land, but said application was denied.

That your petitioner is the uncle of said passenger and makes this petition on his behalf.

Wherefore, your petitioner prays that a writ of habeas corpus may be granted direct to the said Master, commanding him to have the body of said passenger before your Honor, at a time and place therein to be specified, to do and receive what shall then and there be considered by your Honor concering him, together with the time and cause of his detention, and said writ; and that he may be restored to his liberty.

Dated on the 29 day of July 1890

Ching Quong 陳廣達 Ark *Petitioner.*

STATE OF CALIFORNIA, CITY AND COUNTY OF SAN FRANCISCO, Northern District of California, United States of America. } ss

Ching Quong Ark being duly sworn, says that he is the Petitioner above named, and that he has heard read the foregoing petition, and knows the contents thereof and that the same is true of his own knowledge, that he is a merchant residing and doing business in the firm of Wa Yuen Chung No. 769 Clay Street.

Sworn to before me this 29 day of July 1890

Ching Quong 陳廣達 Ark

Commissioner of the Circuit Court of the United States for the Northern District of California.

黄焜铨 (Wong Quoon Sin or Wong Goon Seen) was born in 1869 on a farm leased from Joseph Cone. In 1890, his uncle Chin Quong of Wa Yuen Chung testified that he was born in the United States, and his father, Wong Shoon, was a partner at the Quong Hing Wah Company, located at No. 10 (710/824) High Street in Red Bluff. (Frederick Bee Project.)

余女女本 (Yee Ah Moy) was born in 1866 at the Kwong Hing Lung Company to Jean Ah Haw (Jung Shee). His father, Yee Lin Din, was a partner of the Quong Hing Wah Company located at No. 10 (710/824) High Street in Red Bluff. In 1891, Ah Moy returned to America and had Yee Tye testify on his behalf. (Frederick Bee Project.)

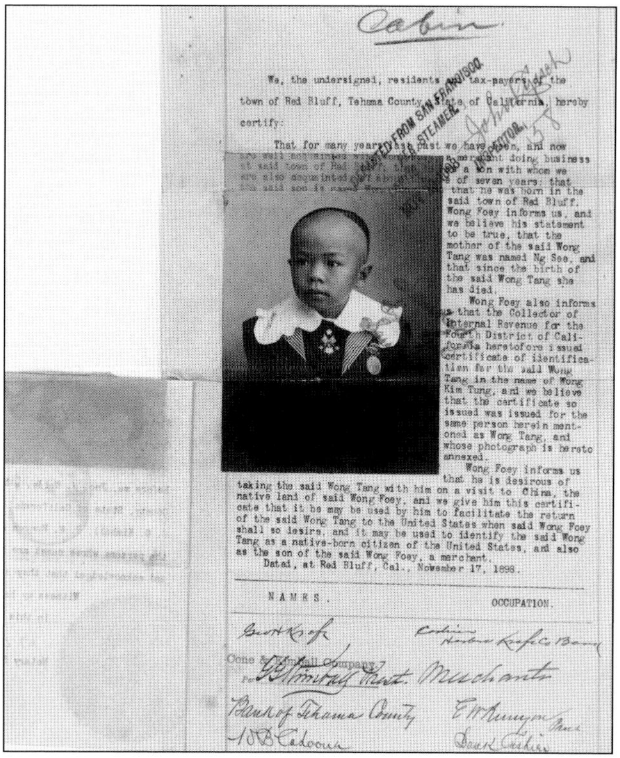

Cabin

We, the undersigned, residents and tax-payers of the town of Red Bluff, Tehama County, State of California, hereby certify:

That for many years last past we have been, and now are well acquainted with [illegible], a merchant doing business at said town of Red Bluff; that [illegible] a son with whom we are also acquainted [illegible] of seven years; that the said son is named [illegible] that he was born in the said town of Red Bluff. Wong Foey informs us, and we believe his statement to be true, that the mother of the said Wong Tang was named Ng See, and that since the birth of the said Wong Tang she has died.

Wong Foey also informs us that the Collector of Internal Revenue for the Fourth District of California heretofore issued certificate of identification for the said Wong Tang in the name of Wong Kim Tung, and we believe that the certificate so issued was issued for the same person herein mentioned as Wong Tang, and whose photograph is hereto annexed.

Wong Foey informs us that he is desirous of taking the said Wong Tang with him on a visit to China, the native land of said Wong Foey, and we give him this certificate that it he may be used by him to facilitate the return of the said Wong Tang to the United States when said Wong Foey shall so desire, and it may be used to identify the said Wong Tang as a native-born citizen of the United States, and also as the son of the said Wong Foey, a merchant.

Dated, at Red Bluff, Cal., November 17, 1898.

NAMES.	OCCUPATION.
Geo H Kraft	Cashier Herbert Kraft Co Bank
G G Kimball	Merchant
Bank of Tehama County	E W Runyon Pres
W B Cahoone	Bank Cashier

Even though Tang Foey was born in Red Bluff, he was still required to carry a Certificate of Identification. In 1893, Wong Foey took his three-year-old son, Wong Gim Tang (Tang Foey), to China, where his mother died. Prominent friends such as Geo H. Kraft, G.G. Kimball, E.W. Runyon, and W.B. Cahoone signed notarized testimonies for his overseas trips.

In 1899, Chin Sam testified for his nephew Too You Fook (Dr. Chew Yuen). Upon arrival, Too You Fook waited on the steamer but was detained at the San Francisco wharf mail dock when a cheat sheet addressed to his uncle was intercepted. With the help of an expensive lawyer, he was eventually released for having no knowledge of the cheat sheet, having never received it.

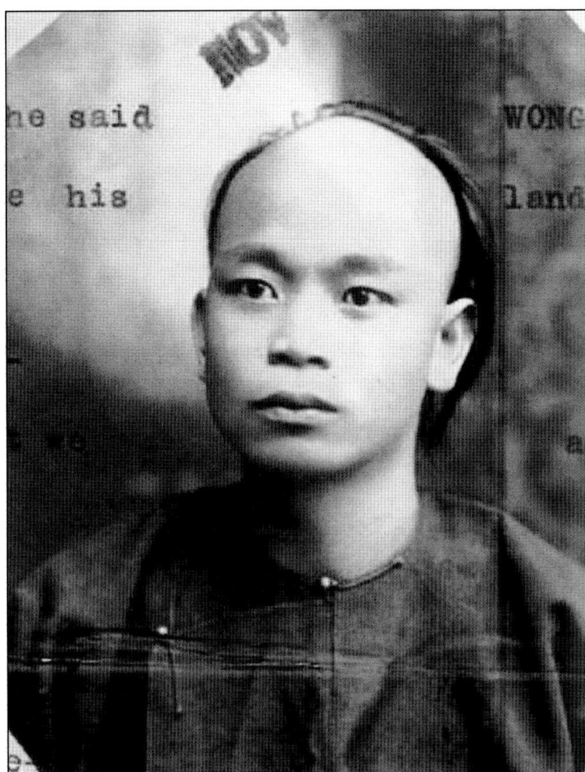

In 1899, business owner Wong Gung Say took his son Wong Wing to China. When his son returned in 1901, Wong Wing was denied entry into America despite written testimony from merchant friends Oroville Pate, A.H. Hoffman, Geo. W. Vestal, Quong Hi, and Tung Hep, stating he was born in Red Bluff and worked at Quong Hi Laundry, located on Main Street.

Unlike most, when Lim Toy returned to America in 1903, he landed at the San Francisco wharf mail dock without issue. Lim Toy was born June 5, 1878, in Red Bluff to Mrs. Lim Seen Oh (Chung Shee) and Mr. Lim Shin Jeung Gim. Both of his parents returned to China to operate the Hai Yick (Hai Heng) and Company in Sun Chung City, which had over 200 residents at the time.

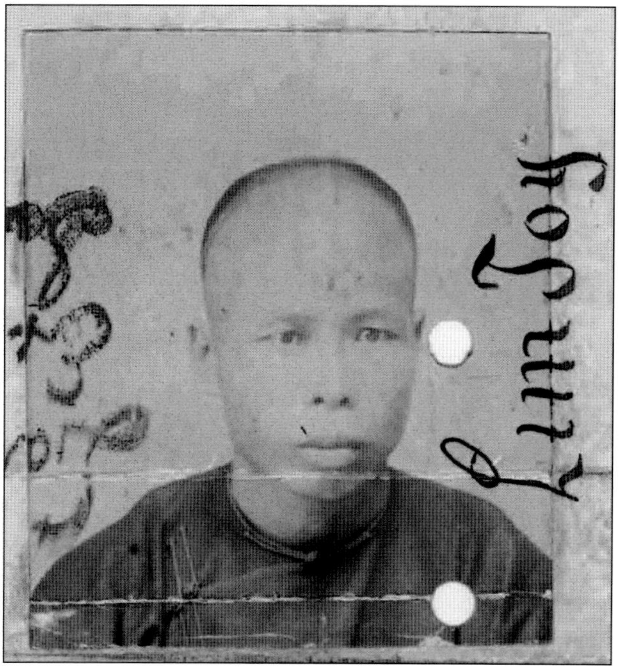

Form 461 [TRIPLICATE]

APPLICATION OF LAWFULLY DOMICILED CHINESE MERCHANT, TEACHER, OR STUDENT, FOR PREINVESTIGATION OF STATUS

Department of Commerce and Labor
IMMIGRATION SERVICE

Office of

Port of San Francisco,

October 1., 1912.

To Commissioner of Immigration, Chinese and Immigrant Inspector, San Francisco Cal.

Sir: It being my intention to leave the United States on a temporary visit abroad, and to depart and return through the Chinese port of entry of San Francisco, I hereby apply, under the provisions of Rule 15 of the Regulations of the Department of Commerce and Labor, for preinvestigation of my claimed status as a lawfully domiciled merchant

I submit herewith the names of two (or more) "credible witnesses other than Chinese" who can testify of their own knowledge that for at least one year immediately preceding the date of this application I have been engaged in the occupation of a Merchant, and have not performed any manual labor except such as was necessary in the conduct of my said occupation. I am prepared to appear personally and to produce before you at such time and place as you may designate the said witnesses and (if a merchant) the partnership or other books of the firm in which I claim membership.

The names and addresses of my witnesses are:
A. L. Conard, Tremont Hotel, Red Bluff
W. H. Fisher, 707 Main St., " "

TO BE FILLED OUT IF MERCHANT

The firm in which I claim membership is known as Jok Kee & Company

Address No. 866 Rio St. City Red Bluff State California

My partners in said business are as set forth in the partnership list of our firm filed - No list filed

My interest therein amounts to $ ~~1000.00~~ $500.00 and was acquired more than two years ago 19

It is not my intention to dispose of such interest while absent from the United States. During the entire year last past I have performed no manual labor other than that necessary to the conduct of the said mercantile business.

TO BE FILLED OUT IF TEACHER OR STUDENT

~~I have been engaged during the entire year last past in the occupation of teaching or studying (name branches taught or studied)~~

at the following place or places
and during the said time have not engaged in the performance of manual labor.

Signature in Chinese 黃江

Signature in English Wong Gong

Address 866 Rio St, Red Bluff Cal.

Height 5 feet 3 1/2 inches

Physical marks or peculiarities None. Bald Head.

Subscribed and sworn to before me, this 6th day of November 1912.

Jno. J. Wells, Notary Public.

Port of SAN FRANCISCO

DEC 1 0 1912 191

Respectfully returned to Commissioner of Immigration, Port of San Francisco.
Chinese and Immigrant Inspector.

With the information that I am ___ prepared, on the basis of the evidence submitted with the original of this application, to approve said application.

(Signed) Samuel W. Backus
Commissioner of Immigration or Inspector in Charge.

11-170

Wong was interrogated due to an adjoining hallway with a neighboring building. Upon Wong Gong's arrival in 1912, he was detained while the Department of Commerce and Labor inspector verified that his store, Jok Kee Company, was leased from Arthur L. Conard, located at 866 High Street in Red Bluff. W.H. Fisher even gave a strong testimony that Wong shopped at their grocery store located at 707 Main Street.

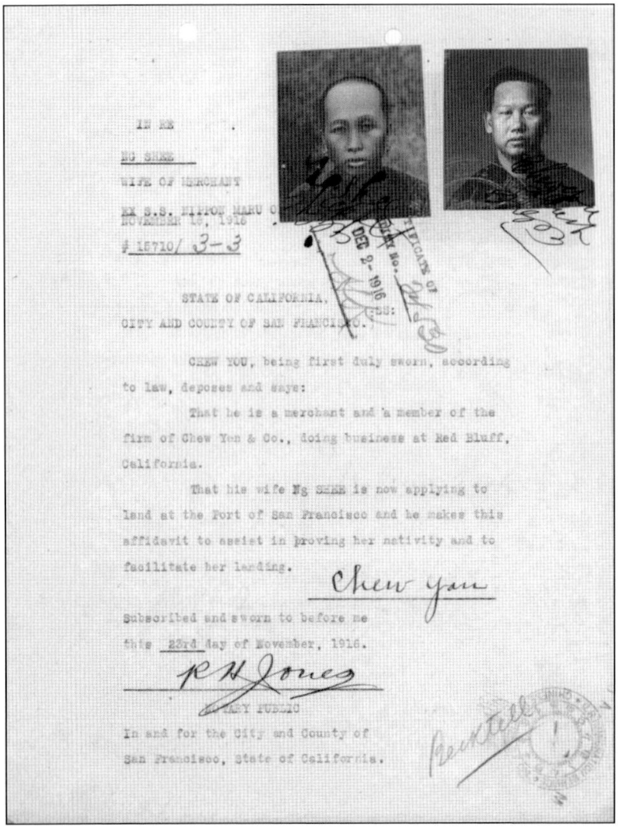

IN RE

NG SHEE

WIFE OF MERCHANT

EX S.S. NIPPON MARU O
NOVEMBER [illegible], 1916

15710/ 3-3

STATE OF CALIFORNIA,
CITY AND COUNTY OF SAN FRANCISCO. } SS:

CHEW YOU, being first duly sworn, according to law, deposes and says:

That he is a merchant and a member of the firm of Chew Yen & Co., doing business at Red Bluff, California.

That his wife Ng SHEE is now applying to land at the Port of San Francisco and he makes this affidavit to assist in proving her nativity and to facilitate her landing.

Chew You

Subscribed and sworn to before me this 23rd day of November, 1916.

R H Jones
NOTARY PUBLIC
In and for the City and County of San Francisco, State of California.

In 1914, J.A. Owens helped Chew You obtain his merchant status from the Department of Labor in Sacramento. Chew You (right) was relocating his wife, Ng Shee (left), and their two sons: biological son Chew Pack Lan and nephew Chew Pack Quoy, to join him in Red Bluff. His wife, Ng Shee, was pregnant with their second child, Violet (Chew) Dong.

Chew Pack Lan (Dick Chew) immigrated as a student of a merchant's son. The plan was for the Chew family to enter the land of opportunity through San Francisco's Angel Island and live at the Chew Yuen Company as one large family.

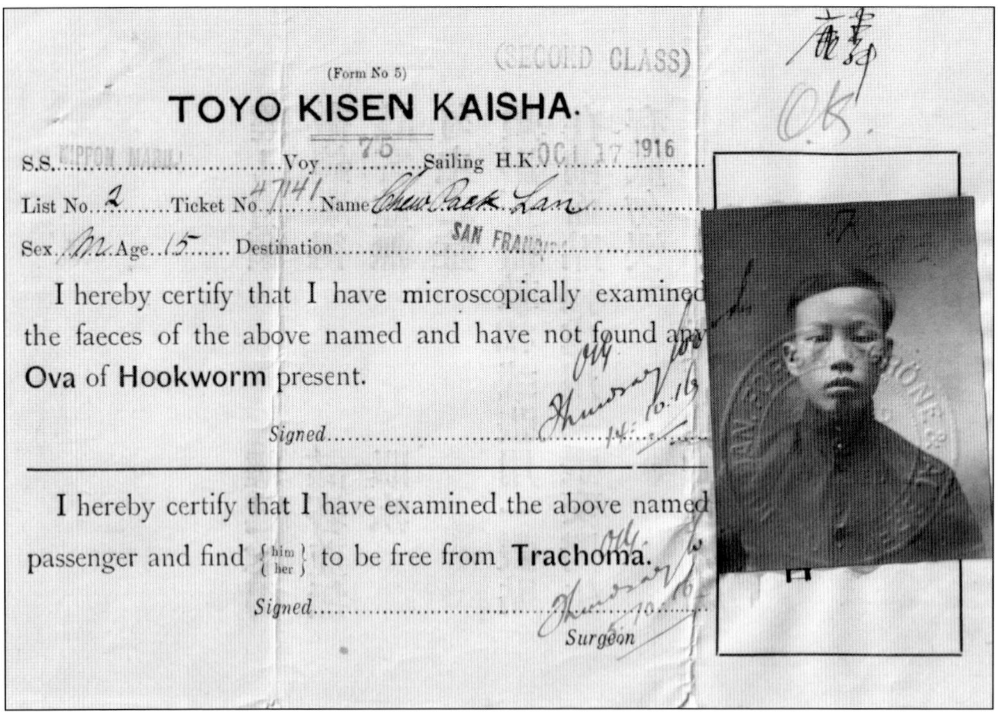

(SECOND CLASS)

(Form No 5)

TOYO KISEN KAISHA.

S.S. NIPPON MARU Voy 75 Sailing H.K. OCT 17 1916

List No. 2 Ticket No. 47141 Name Chew Pack Lan

Sex M Age 15 Destination SAN FRANCISCO

I hereby certify that I have microscopically examined the faeces of the above named and have not found any Ova of Hookworm present.

Signed ....

I hereby certify that I have examined the above named passenger and find {him / her} to be free from Trachoma.

Signed ....
Surgeon

Chew Pack Lan (Bock Quee, Chew Quoy Park, or Ned Chew) had varying birthdays from January 5, 1899, to November 24, 1897. He attended Gee Hang School and Ngee Young School in preparation for immigrating to the United States with his uncle Chew You, who was reported as his father to appeal to the immigration officers.

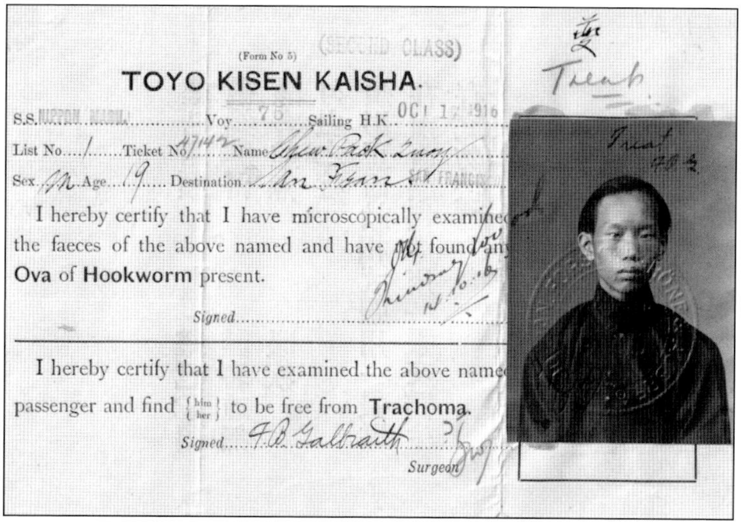

(Form No 5) (SECOND CLASS)

TOYO KISEN KAISHA.

S.S. NIPPON MARU Voy. 75 Sailing H.K. OCT 1 1916

List No. 1 Ticket No. 4714 Name Chew Pack Quoy

Sex M Age 19 Destination San Francisco

I hereby certify that I have microscopically examined the faeces of the above named and have not found any Ova of Hookworm present.

Signed

I hereby certify that I have examined the above named passenger and find {him/her} to be free from Trachoma.

Signed F.B. Galbraith Surgeon

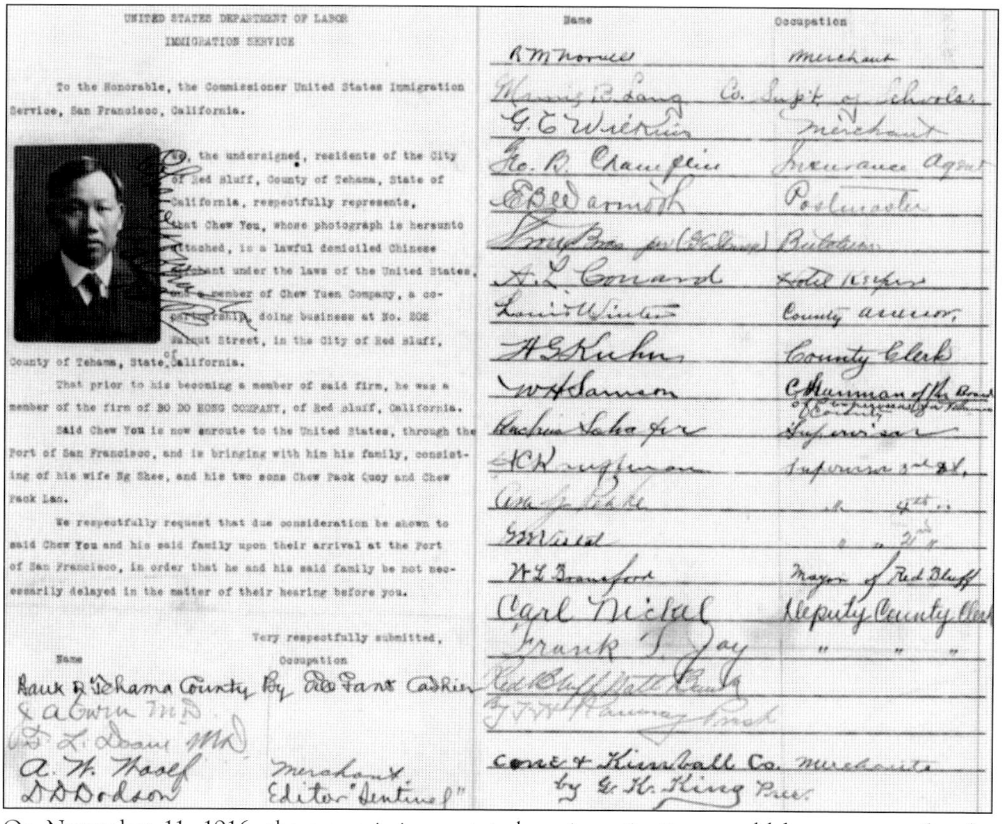

UNITED STATES DEPARTMENT OF LABOR

IMMIGRATION SERVICE

To the Honorable, the Commissioner United States Immigration Service, San Francisco, California.

We, the undersigned, residents of the City of Red Bluff, County of Tehama, State of California, respectfully represents, that Chew You, whose photograph is hereunto attached, is a lawful domiciled Chinese merchant under the laws of the United States, and a member of Chew Yuen Company, a co-partnership, doing business at No. 202 Walnut Street, in the City of Red Bluff, County of Tehama, State of California.

That prior to his becoming a member of said firm, he was a member of the firm of BO DO HONG COMPANY, of Red Bluff, California.

Said Chew You is now enroute to the United States, through the Port of San Francisco, and is bringing with him his family, consisting of his wife Ng Shee, and his two sons Chew Pack Quoy and Chew Pack Lan.

We respectfully request that due consideration be shown to said Chew You and his said family upon their arrival at the Port of San Francisco, in order that he and his said family be not necessarily delayed in the matter of their hearing before you.

Very respectfully submitted,

Name	Occupation
Bank of Tehama County By [illegible] Cashier	
[illegible] M.D.	
[illegible] M.D.	
A. W. Thoelf	Merchant
D.D. Dodson	Editor "Sentinel"
R.M. Norvell	Merchant
[illegible]	Co. Supt. of Schools
G. C. Wilkins	Merchant
Geo. R. Champlin	Insurance Agent
E.B. Dearmoth	Postmaster
[illegible] Bros.	Butchers
A. L. Conard	Hotel Keeper
Louis Winter	County Assessor
H.G. Kuhn	County Clerk
W.H. Samson	Chairman of the Board of Supervisors of Tehama County
[illegible]	Supervisor
[illegible]	Supervisor 3rd Dist.
[illegible]	" 4th "
[illegible]	" " 2nd
W.L. Bransford	Mayor of Red Bluff
Carl Nickel	Deputy County Clerk
Frank T. Jay	" " "
Red Bluff Natl Bank By [illegible] Pres.	
Cone & Kimball Co. by G. H. King Pres.	Merchants

On November 11, 1916, the commissioner stated no investigation would be necessary for the Chew family after receiving this petition from attorney W.A. Fish. The petition was a powerful statement with 20 prominent leaders, such as the mayor and postmaster from Red Bluff, asking for the commissioner of the US Immigration Service in San Francisco to give due consideration to the Chew family upon their arrival on November 24, 1916.

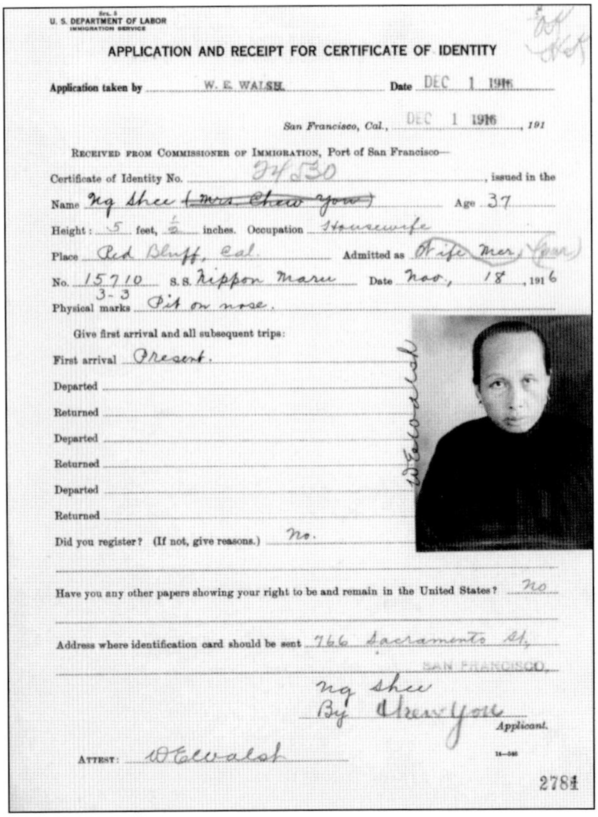

U. S. DEPARTMENT OF LABOR
IMMIGRATION SERVICE

APPLICATION AND RECEIPT FOR CERTIFICATE OF IDENTITY

Application taken by W. E. WALSH. Date DEC 1 1916

San Francisco, Cal., DEC 1 1916, 191

Received from Commissioner of Immigration, Port of San Francisco—

Certificate of Identity No. 24530, issued in the

Name Ng Shee ~~(Mrs Chew You)~~ Age 37

Height: 5 feet, 2 inches. Occupation Housewife

Place Red Bluff, Cal. Admitted as Wife Mer.

No. 15710 3-3 S.S. Nippon Maru Date Nov. 18, 1916

Physical marks Pit on nose.

Give first arrival and all subsequent trips:

First arrival Present.

Departed

Returned

Departed

Returned

Departed

Returned

Did you register? (If not, give reasons.) No.

Have you any other papers showing your right to be and remain in the United States? No

Address where identification card should be sent 766 Sacramento St, SAN FRANCISCO.

Ng Shee
By Chew You
Applicant.

Attest: WEWalsh

2784

Despite the best efforts from prominent men of Red Bluff, pregnant Ng Shee and her family were detained at the Angel Island incarceration center and subjected to harsh interrogations, as can be seen through the exhaustion expressed in this picture. Their detention was due to a mismatched answer from her nephew Ned Chew regarding the location of a water buffalo and the placement of a picture. They were eventually released.

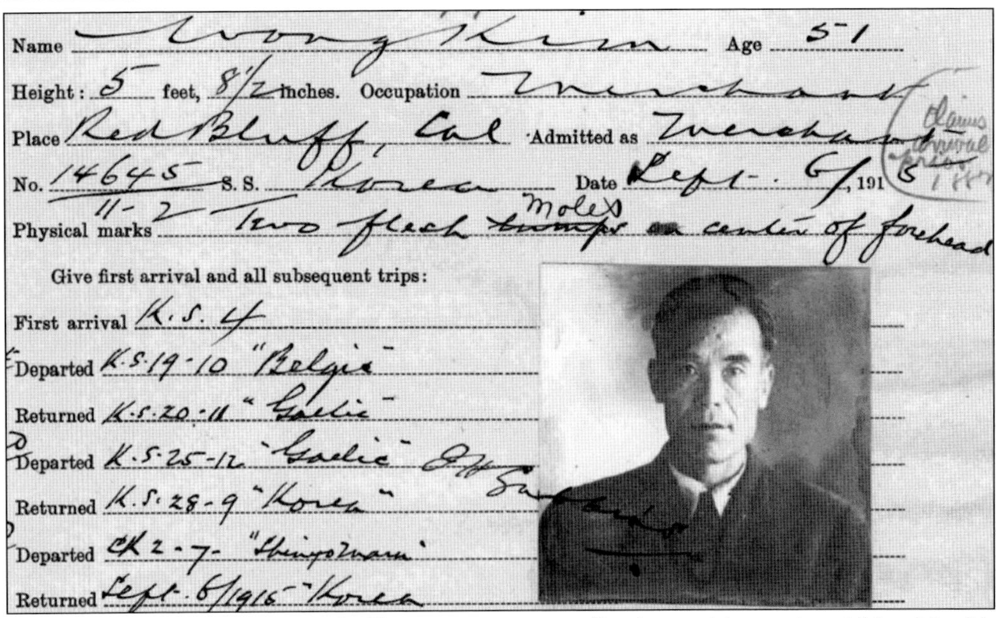

Name Wong Kim Age 51

Height: 5 feet, 8 1/2 inches. Occupation Merchant

Place Red Bluff, Cal Admitted as Merchant

No. 14645 11-2 S.S. Korea Date Sept. 6, 1916

Physical marks Two flesh ~~lumps~~ moles on center of forehead

Give first arrival and all subsequent trips:

First arrival K.S. 4

Departed K.S. 19-10 "Belgic"

Returned K.S. 20-11 "Gaelic"

Departed K.S. 25-12 "Gaelic"

Returned K.S. 28-9 "Korea"

Departed CK 2-7- "Shinyo Maru"

Returned Sept. 6/1916 "Korea"

In 1915, Wong Kim was accused of having uncinariasis (hookworm) by an Angel Island health inspector. He had to pay a $50 advance deposit and $1.25 per day for his healthcare that totaled $7.50 by the time of his release. As a partner of the Quong Ying Low Company, located at 814 High Street in Red Bluff since 1893, he received a monthly salary of $25.

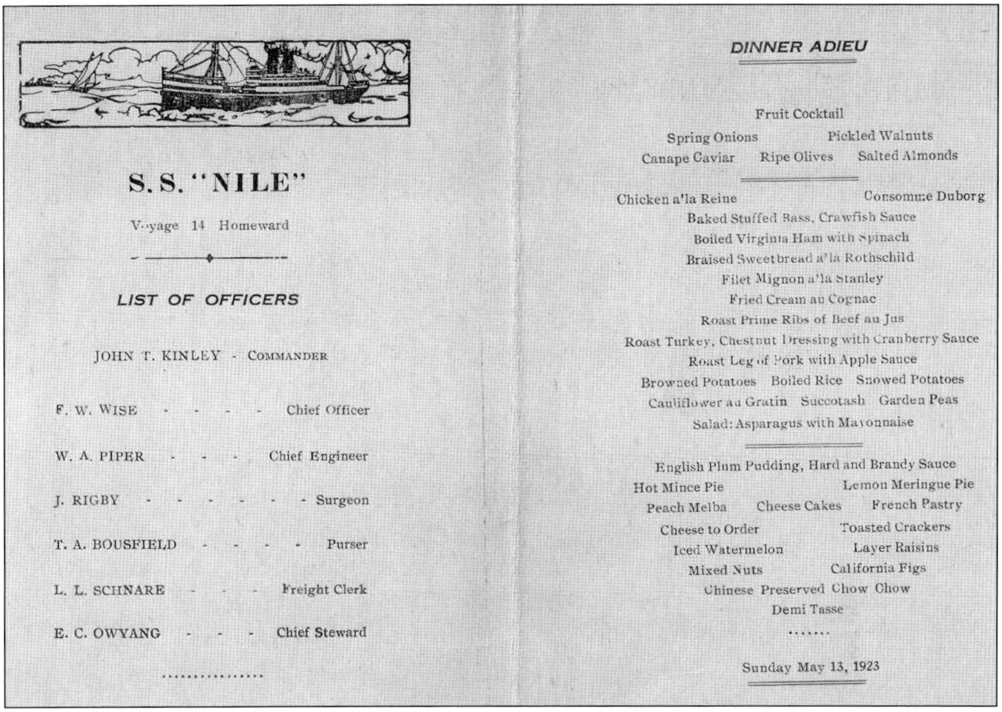

S. S. "NILE"

Voyage 14 Homeward

LIST OF OFFICERS

JOHN T. KINLEY - COMMANDER

F. W. WISE - - - - - Chief Officer

W. A. PIPER - - - - Chief Engineer

J. RIGBY - - - - - - - - Surgeon

T. A. BOUSFIELD - - - - - Purser

L. L. SCHNARE - - - - Freight Clerk

E. C. OWYANG - - - - Chief Steward

DINNER ADIEU

Fruit Cocktail
Spring Onions Pickled Walnuts
Canape Caviar Ripe Olives Salted Almonds

Chicken a'la Reine Consomme Duborg
Baked Stuffed Bass, Crawfish Sauce
Boiled Virginia Ham with Spinach
Braised Sweetbread a'la Rothschild
Filet Mignon a'la Stanley
Fried Cream au Cognac
Roast Prime Ribs of Beef au Jus
Roast Turkey, Chestnut Dressing with Cranberry Sauce
Roast Leg of Pork with Apple Sauce
Browned Potatoes Boiled Rice Snowed Potatoes
Cauliflower au Gratin Succotash Garden Peas
Salad: Asparagus with Mayonnaise

English Plum Pudding, Hard and Brandy Sauce
Hot Mince Pie Lemon Meringue Pie
Peach Melba Cheese Cakes French Pastry
Cheese to Order Toasted Crackers
Iced Watermelon Layer Raisins
Mixed Nuts California Figs
Chinese Preserved Chow Chow
Demi Tasse

Sunday May 13, 1923

After her arranged marriage to Dick Chew in 台山縣 浮石村 (Fow Shek), 陳順蘭 Chin See (Suon Lon Chin), bravely embarked on a journey to America in 1923. Despite obstacles like the Page Act, she immigrated while carrying her first child, Julia Chew in her womb. Pictured above is the dinner menu for the SS *Nile* steamship, and below is Chin See, her sister 陳順速 Suon Len, who married Doon Ping Moy.

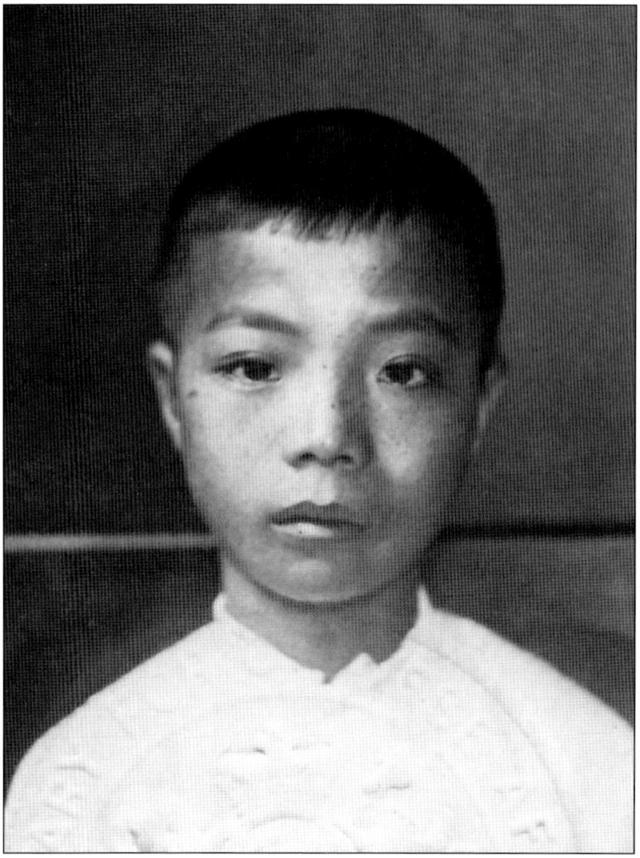

陳想華 (Henry Chin, or Chin Theung Wah) was born in 1920 at Ai Wan Village, Toishan, China. In 1931, Henry journeyed across the Pacific and then crossed the Canadian border by train and ship to Boston. He was tagged and treated like cargo. As a child, he learned his father's laundry business, located at 147 East Merrimack Street in Lowell, Massachusetts. (Chin family.)

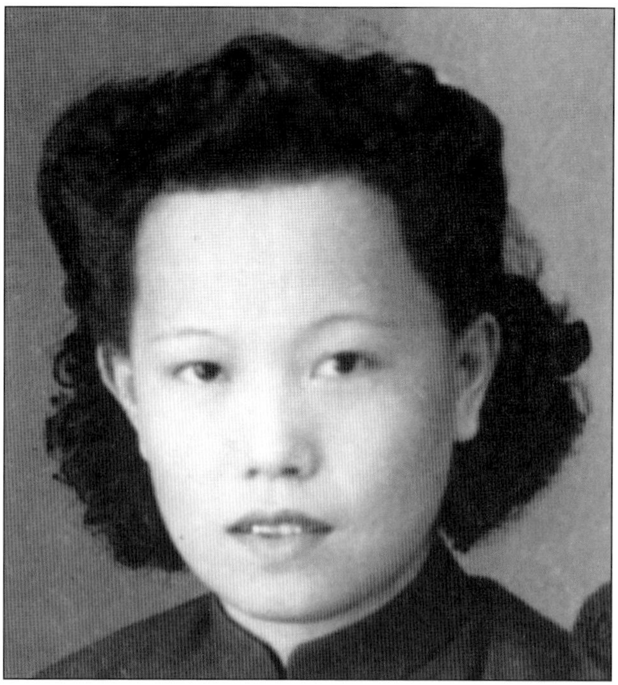

In 1927, Henry married Lai Chew (Debbie Lai Chin), born in 1927 in 台山縣 浮石村 (Fow Shek, Toishan), China. Under the War Brides Act, Lai was able to immigrate in 1948 to Red Bluff, where she started a family. She was very proud of becoming a naturalized citizen in 1971 and was active in the local church. (Chin family.)

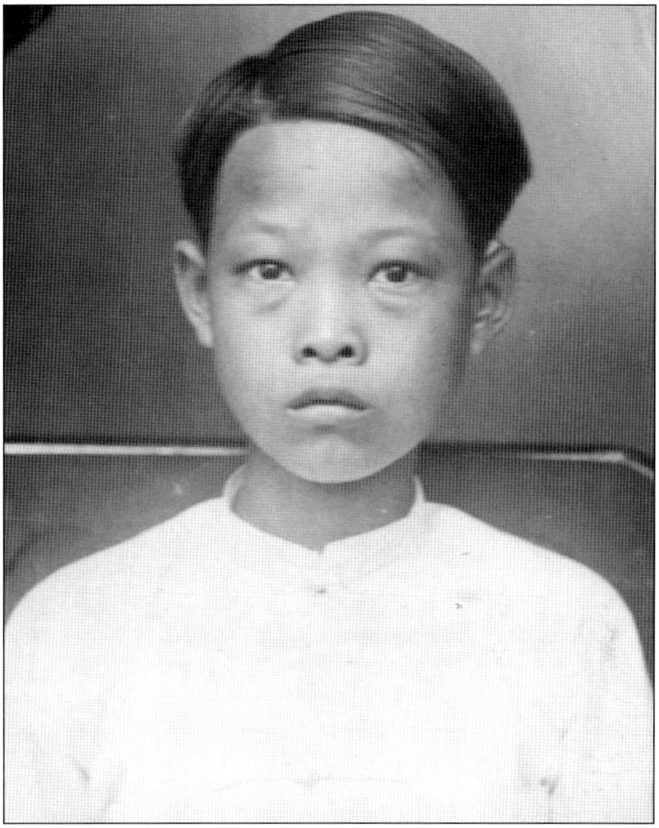

Albert Git Lee Chan was born on June 15, 1915, in Loong Gong Li Village, 開平市 (Hoiping), China. His biological father was Chin Moy. After Albert's father died, he had to immigrate, reporting his uncle as his father. Albert's biological older brother, Chin Bock Sai, was born in 1894 and lived in America with his father until he was deported in 1918 for physical defects. (Janet Chan.)

Pictured in 1939 is a Public Health Inspection card from Hong Kong that was required before voyaging to America on the President Coolidge steamship. Mrs. May Yuk (Seeto) Jung married Mr. Lew Jung (Lie Jung, Hei Shoon, or Fong Shew Ming) of Willows. Their children were Fong Ming, Lew Wai Jang, and Lew Wai (Jang) Yee. (Lew and Fong families.)

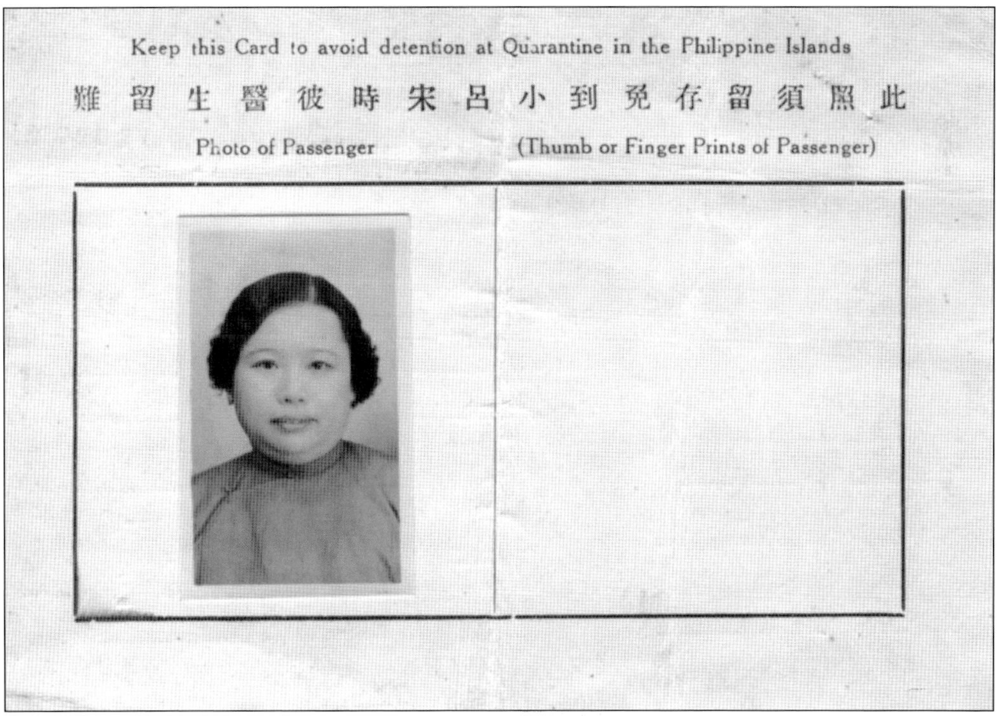

Keep this Card to avoid detention at Quarantine in the Philippine Islands

此照須留存免到小呂宋時彼醫生留難

Photo of Passenger

(Thumb or Finger Prints of Passenger)

Marion (Poy) Shu and Grace (Poy) Yuen Gan (right) were siblings. Due to the Great Depression, their father, George Poy, relocated his family to China during the Second Sino-Japanese War. Marion would return to the United States using War Department channels in 1944, while Grace moved with Letitia Frances Po-Wen Huang (Bo Do Hong) to Red Bluff in 1940, where she would meet her first husband, Dr. Chew Owen Yuen. (Wei-ling [Yuen] Louie.)

Wong Tze Yen Poy briefly resided in Red Bluff after returning to America from China as a non-quota immigrant in September 1951, following the introduction of Bill 124 to the 52nd US Congress on January 8, 1951. From left to right are (first row) Martha Toy, William Toy Jr. (Jeepe Toy), Wei-ling (Yuen) Louie, Darryl Dong, and Bruce Chin; (second row) Wong Tze Yen Poy, Le-ren Yuen, and Lai (Chew) Chin. (Chin family.)

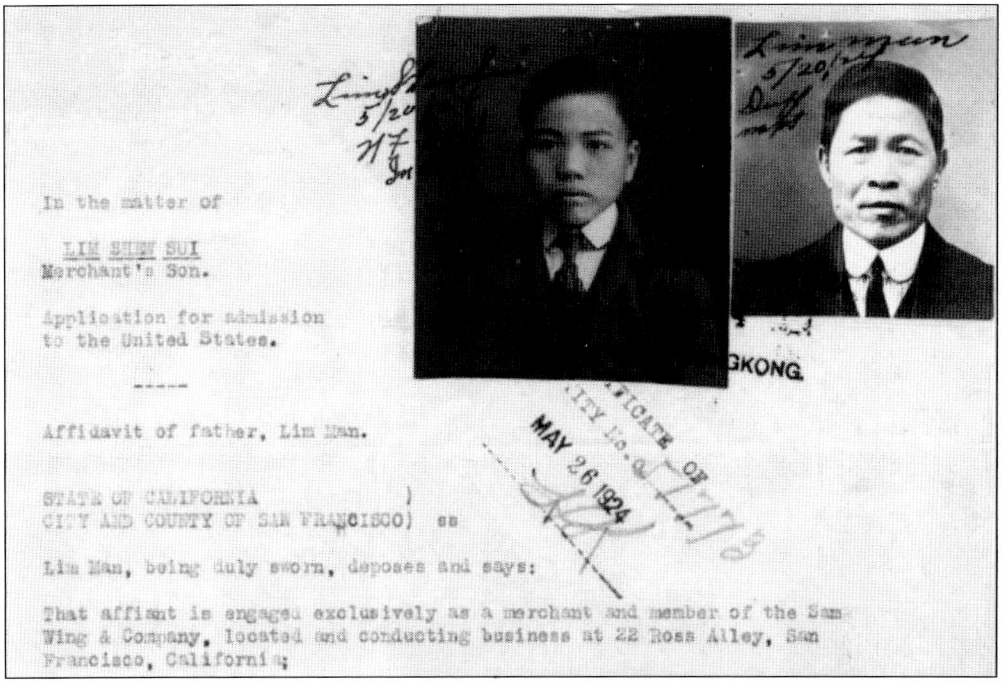

In the matter of

LIM SHEW SUI
Merchant's Son.

Application for admission
to the United States.

Affidavit of father, Lim Man.

STATE OF CALIFORNIA)
CITY AND COUNTY OF SAN FRANCISCO) ss

Lim Man, being duly sworn, deposes and says:

That affiant is engaged exclusively as a merchant and member of the Sam Wing & Company, located and conducting business at 22 Ross Alley, San Francisco, California;

MAY 26 1924

On May 20, 1924, Peter Lim (Lim Shew Sui, Lem Suey, or Lim Tung Wah) needed to remember that his identity from this point forward would be Lim Shew Sui, who was born on November 22, 1911. Lim Man (Yee Kim Sing) needed additional workers at his restaurants and claimed Peter as his son. Kim Sing also brought his biological son Willie (Lim Shew Sun), born on December 5, 1910.

Due to the Chinese Exclusion Act of 1882, Peter Lim did not meet his firstborn, Pattie Lim, until she was 10 years old in 1947. When the Chinese Alien Wives of American Citizens Act was implemented, Peter quickly brought his wife and daughter to America, where they settled in Redding, California. Pictured are May Lim, Pattie Lim, Ronnie Lim, and Peter Lim at Yen's Chinese Laundry. (Jeannie Lim.)

In 1936, fourteen-year-old Mee Ning Fong, son of Fong Kee You and Chin Yoak May, walked two miles in 兩洞鄉 (Leung Tung Village), 台山 (Toisan), in Guangdong Province to board a tiny steamboat to Bok Kia. Continuing his journey to America, from Bok Kai, he traveled on another steamboat embarking for Hong Kong, where they prepared for his US immigration on the *President Pierce* steamship.

World War II resulted in the repeal of the Chinese Exclusion Act, ending the ban on naturalization for Chinese immigrants, and it was a joyous event. Pictured with his naturalization certificate is Dick Chew, who immigrated to the United States at 14 years old. He practiced for the exam with his children day and night, and his family commemorated the day with an American flag cake made by Grace (Poy) [Yuen] Gan.

Three

20th-Century Chinese American Descendants

The Chinese community in the twentieth century was deeply impacted by the Chinese Exclusion Act of 1882. The law was particularly devastating for the population of Chinese women, as it limited their migration. Moreover, in 1880, the California Civil Code Section 60 prohibited interracial marriages between white persons, "negros," "mulattos," or Mongolians. The continuing restrictions on immigration and interracial marriages resulted in the decline of the US Chinese population from approximately 107,000 in 1890 to a low of 61,000 by 1920. The population would not begin to rise again until after 1965.

The offspring of Tehama County's Chinese pioneers brought forth the first generation of American-born Chinese who faced a unique challenge in their upbringing. Chinese Americans were now considered old-fashioned by newcomers from bustling areas such as Hong Kong. Meanwhile, as they attended non-segregated public schools in Tehama County, their assimilation into Western culture resulted in many losing their ability to speak or read Chinese characters. For those living in Red Bluff's Chinatown, Dr. Chew, Yuen hired a private tutor, Ma Gong Wong, followed by Stanford University graduate James Yuan in 1939 to teach Chinese School on weekends. The children were provided a Chinese education, learning traditional calligraphy, speaking Cantonese, and reading classic works such as the Great Learning, Doctrine of the Mean, Analects, and Mencius. Many incorporated Western traditions into their daily lives by celebrating the Winter Festival with Western symbols like Christmas trees alongside ancestral offerings such as sweet dumplings and rice wine. For many, the first generation of American-born Chinese would grow up in the restaurant business. Later, as the Chinese community found professional work and achieved financial success, they began to move out of the once-segregated Chinatowns to new suburbs or other outlying neighborhoods, impacting the New World in a new way.

In 1947, what remained of Red Bluff's Chinatown was scheduled to be demolished. The Chew family would be evicted and quickly purchased the Roosevelt Café located at 860 Main Street. The Roosevelt Café had been operated by Yee Kim Sing since 1934, known for his signature cuisines such as chop suey, chow mein, and hot chicken. He rented the upstairs living quarters to Yee Wong Sing, Hang Yee, and Ting Sun Quong.

Seated at the table's center in a plaid jacket is *koon sok* (叔 elder) George Wing. He lived alone in the former Canton Café, a Chinese and Mexican restaurant run by Yee Wing, at 832 High Street, Red Bluff, California. George worked as a hotel janitor until Chinatown's demolition in 1948 left him displaced. He sought shelter in the Ming Terrace Restaurant's basement but was forced to relocate.

After the Chew family took their savings from the California Café pinball machine to buy the Roosevelt Café, they had a large grand opening, renaming it the Ming Terrace Restaurant. Pictured from left to right are John Chew Young, Mary Lee Young, and Dick Chew. John was the president of Wing Nien Soy Sauce Manufacturing Co., the first producer of soy sauce in the United States.

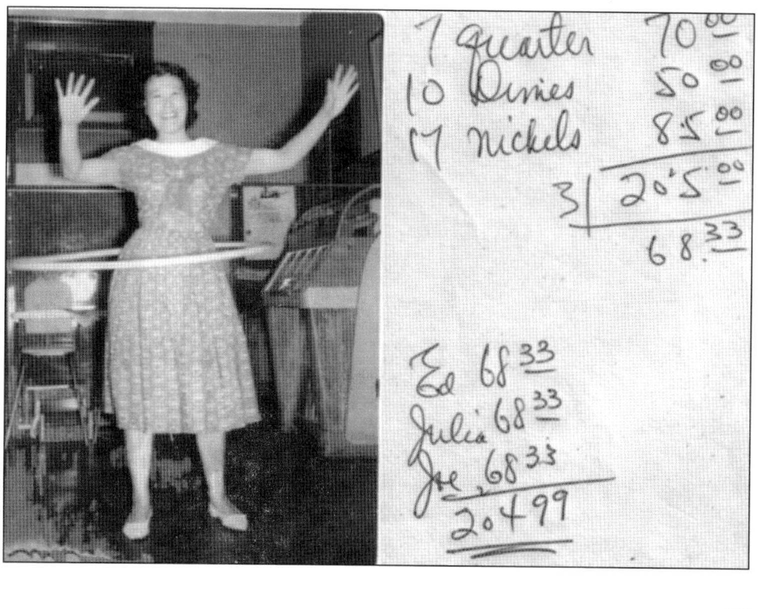

The Ming Terrace Restaurant was the last restaurant to operate in Red Bluff's Chinatown. Like most Chinese American restaurants, it is fondly remembered for its jukebox machines that were on lease, where a portion of the proceeds went to the restaurant owner. Payroll was split equally among the family regardless of employment title.

Thanksgiving and Christmas are joyful holidays for all households. Dick Chew is pictured on the second floor of the Ming Terrace Restaurant, taking a break from the restaurant business and setting the table for his family to celebrate Christmas.

Although rare, Red Bluff's Chinatown had a professional Chinese photographer for family portraits. From left to right are (first row) Dr. Kenneth Chew, Jim Chew, and Christopher Chew; (second row) Jane (Chew) Jung, Violet (Chew) Dong, Mrs. Ng Shee Chew, Dick Chew, and wife Chin See Chew; (third row) Nettie (Chew) Ong, Edward Chew, Joe Chew, Julia Chew, and Hazel (Chew) Wong.

In this picture, Violet (Chew) Dong is standing in front of 838 High Street and Walnut Street in Red Bluff's Chinatown. By the 1940s, only three of the original wooden commercial buildings with living quarters in the rear remained parallel to the Sacramento River.

Joe You Chew was born at the Chew Yuen Company in Red Bluff. He is pictured here outside the Japanese women's boardinghouse, where he later recalled seeing the residents taken to internment camps during World War II. At the onset of the Great Depression, Joe began cooking at the California Café at just nine years old. Throughout elementary school and beyond, he excelled as a star athlete in both basketball and tennis. He attended the University of California, Berkeley, until World War II, and later graduated from California State University, Chico, with a degree in accounting.

On January 15, 1907, Dr. Bo Do Hong arranged the first Chinese American wedding in the Chew family, deviating from ancient Chinese traditions. J.A. Owen orchestrated the day, hosting the wedding at the home of her daughter, Letitia Francis Owen, with Presbyterian reverend James Henry Sharp to officiate. This forever changed the Chew family marital traditions for the generations that followed. (Presbyterian Church of Red Bluff.)

Dr. Kenneth Chew is pictured marrying May Wong in 1958. Together, they created influential change at the Chinese Baptist Church in Seattle, Washington. Both graduated from the University of Washington (UW), with Dr. Chew becoming professor emeritus, director of the Western Regional Aquaculture Center, associate dean of the UW College of Ocean and Fishery Science, and serving as west side commissioner of the Washington Department of Fish & Wildlife.

By the 20th century, the Chinese community wore Western attire. This photograph was used for newspapers advertising the Chew Yuen Company. 趙綬賢 Dr. Chew Yuen's papers stated he was 曹有福 born at 754 Washington Street in San Francisco on April 28, 1870, while his parents were on business traveling as merchants in America. On paper, his father's name was Too Ming, his grandfather was Ho Wing Gum, and his mother was Chin Shee.

Pictured from left to right are (first row) Nettie (Chew) Ong, Chew Fish Yuen (Too Doon Wee), Violet (Chew) Dong, Chew Owen Yuen (Too Chew Owen), and Chew Robert Yuen (Robert Bo Do Hong or Too Suey Wee); (second row) Letitia Frances Po-Wen Huang (Bo Do Hong) holding Hazel Yuen (Too Tew Ngon), Margaret Rose Bo Do Hong (Too Gim), and Dr. Chew Yuen holding Chew Cahoone Yuen (Too Gin Wee). (Wei-ling [Yuen] Louie.)

Letitia Frances Bo Do Hong (Frances Too or Too Ngoot) was named after Letitia Francis Owen from Hardinsburg, Kentucky. Letitia Bo Do Hong was born on August 31, 1909, at the Bo Do Hong Company. From left to right are Chung-Chien (Gin) Huang, Letitia Frances Po-Wen Huang (Bo Do Hong), Po-Wen (Baldwin) Huang, Kang-Shih (Rock) Huang, and Po-Wen (Chun-Lin) Huang Jr.

Margaret Rose Bo Do Hong (Too Gim) was born on December 15, 1911, at the Bo Do Hong Company and was married on September 19, 1938, to University of Southern California alumnus and herbalist physician Philip Kimwang Kung (1899–1966) of 839 South Spring Street in Los Angeles, California. Philip had a fatal heart attack while driving in Downtown Los Angeles. (Wei-ling [Yuen] Louie.)

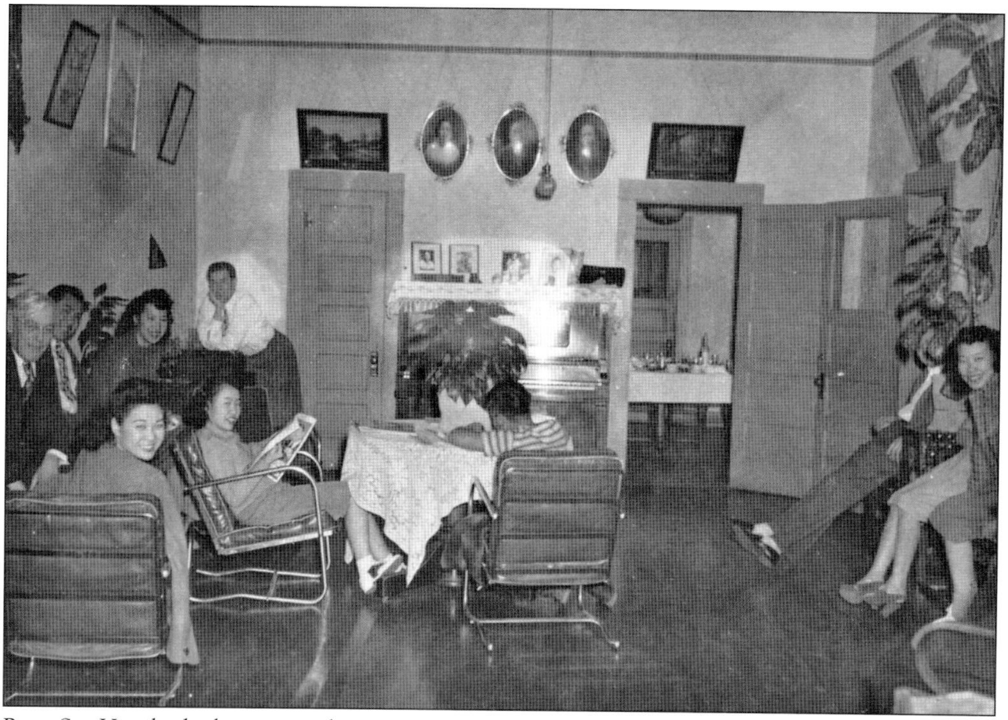

Rose SooHoo had a long courtship with Dr. Chew Fish Yuen. At the time, he was not only considered highly attractive but also a highly sought-after bachelor. Pictured inside the Chew Yuen Company are, from left to right, Rose SooHoo, Emmet Pendleton, Chew Cahoone Yuen, Hazel (Chew) Wong (at the table), Nettie (Chew) Ong, Chew Fish Yuen (in the rear), Joe Chew, Julia Chew, and Dr. Kenneth Chew (at the table).

Hazel (Yuen) Toy (Too Tew Ngon), born on February 10, 1922, at the Chew Yuen Company, was named after Hazel Owen. Hazel's husband, William Kwan Toy Sr., was the son of Dea H. Toy and Lee Chee. Toy opened a grocery store in Phoenix, Arizona, and was able to expand his business by opening what became the popular Shangri-La Restaurant located on Sixteenth Street and Camelback in Phoenix.

Hazel (Yuen) Toy attended the University of California, Berkeley. She had five children: William K. Toy Jr., Douglas K. Toy, Robert C. Toy, Martha (Toy) Wong, and Carol L. Toy. From left to right are Manville Gan, unidentified, Dr. Chew Yuen, unidentified, Hazel (Yuen) Toy, Po-Wen Huang Jr., Letitia Frances Po-Wen Huang (Bo Do Hong), unidentified, Dr. Chew Owen Yuen, Grace (Poy) [Yuen] Gan, Ty-ren Yuen, and Stanford Yuen. (Wei-ling [Yuen] Louie.)

After the Tremont Hotel changed its menu to French cuisine, it no longer employed Chinese chefs. Hence, the Fong family moved and settled in Sacramento, California. Pictured is Edward Fong, son of Jimmy Fong and Lee Mee Gum. (Courtesy of Robert Fong.)

Henry Chin and his family lived at the Fong family's former residence, pictured here, at 831 High Street, later renumbered to 825 High Street in Red Bluff. When the city built its parking lot, it destroyed this section of Chinatown where the Chin family once lived. This loss further an erasure that deepened prejudice by perpetuating tunnel myths that linger to this day. (Chin family.)

Due to the Chin family's forced move, their son would attend Lincoln Street School, Jackson Heights School, and Bidwell School in Red Bluff. Pictured from left to right are Julia Chew, Arleen (Chin) Fadel, Bruce Chin, and Susie (Chin) Guido with her mother, Lai (Chew) Chin, at 950 Cascade Avenue in Red Bluff. (Chin family.)

Bruce Chin, born in 1950 to Henry and Lai Chin, earned a degree in microbiology from California State University, Sacramento. He was a medical technologist for the US Department of Defense and a senior QC associate in biotechnology. In retirement, Bruce dedicated himself to preserving Chinese American heritage by collaborating with numerous historical societies and genealogy research groups. He aided his granduncle Joe Chew in labeling photographs that made this book possible. (Chin family.)

Arleen (Chin) Fadel is Henry and Lai Chin's first daughter, born in Red Bluff in 1952. She graduated from the University of California, Davis, with a degree in scientific and wildlife illustration and retired as a graphic artist. She married Prof. James Fadel, and together, they had two daughters, Monica (Fadel) Berceau and Emma Fadel. (Chin family.)

Born in 1957 in Red Bluff, Susie (Chin) Guido is Henry and Lai Chin's youngest child. She graduated from California State University, Chico, with a degree in graphic design and is a graphic artist. She married James Guido Jr. and has one daughter, Abrianna, and two sons, Nicolino and Sergio. (Chin family.)

Leta's (left) competitive spirit loved mah jong, pai gow, and poker. On April 4, 1920, Leta received an impressive 14,126,420 votes and won a Gulbransen piano in Red Bluff. Leta Dorein Foey (King Hal) was the daughter of Wong Foey and Julia Foey, born on June 13, 1900. She settled in Marysville, California, with her husband, Joe Foe (right), where he was a landlord. (Brian and Lawrence Tom.)

Tang Foey married Hang Yat Yee (Yat Hang Foey), pictured here in preparation for her wedding held on December 26, 1912, at Dr. Joseph A. Owen's home with Rev. A.B. Murphy of the Baptist Church, followed by a Chinese American banquet in Red Bluff's Chinatown. Together, they had 17 children, with 14 surviving to young adulthood. (Valerie Wong.)

The longest-living descendants of Red Bluff's Chinatown were Annie (Foey) Wong, who lived to 103 years old, and Fannie (Foey) Wong, who lived to 104 years old, passing away in 2021; they were Tang Foey's third and fourth of fourteen children. Pictured on the right is Fannie, and her identical twin Annie is on the left, both born on July 28, 1916, in Red Bluff. Annie married Kai Wong, who owned the Sincere Market grocery in San Francisco. (Valerie Wong.)

Pictured here are Annie and Fannie (Foey) Wong. Fannie married World War II veteran Gene Wong. Gene was the second eldest of ten children from Gim and Lee Shee Wong. Gene and his siblings are the founders of a well-known supermarket chain, Bel Air, which was eventually acquired by Raley's Supermarket. Today, Raley's Bel Air supermarket is a major grocery chain throughout Northern California. (Valerie Wong.)

"Slammin'" Sammie Foey was a flyweight class boxer, known as well as Tang Foey's fifth child, born on September 19, 1919, in Red Bluff. In 1935, he won the Amateur Athletic Union Championship and then lost the Golden Gloves in San Francisco to Ray Lunney. Sammie left the ring to pursue his love for fixing cars.

Sammie started his career as an auto mechanic at George Growney's Garage. With his hard work, dedication, and passion for cars, Sammie opened his own auto repair business in Scappoose, Oregon. From left to right are (first row) Henry Foey and Brenda Foey; (second row) Sammie Foey, Fannie (Foey) Wong, Liz Foey, and Dave Foey. (Janine Cheng.)

Tang Foey's daughter Lily was born on November 26, 1913, and married Foon (Tommy) Wing, born September 27, 1911. Their son Ronney Wing is pictured with his wife, Irene Tong, and son Eric Wing. He and Irene settled in San Jose, California. (Eric Wing.)

William Wong Foey is pictured in 2014 with a 10-pound trout in Pyramid Lake, Nevada. Named after his grandfather Wong Foey, William is a multi-talented local educator, fiction author, and abstract artist. His artwork has a unique way of bringing Chinese American history to life through vivid fictional storytelling. (William and Russell Wong Foey.)

Frank and Lee On lived in the rear of the American Café, located at 518 Walnut Street in Red Bluff. Pictured from left to right is their expanded family: (first row) Lee You On, Frank On; (second row) Joseph On, Mabel Anne (On) Foey, John On, Danny On, Louis On, Ronald On, Mary On, and Norma (Wong) On. (William and Russell Wong Foey.)

Danny On was born in Red Bluff's Chinatown and worked at Deschutes National Forest, Kootenai National Forest in Region One, followed by the Flathead National Forest as a silviculturist. He attended California State University, Chico, and the University of Montana, earning a master's degree in forestry in 1952. He coauthored *Plants of Waterton-Glacier National Parks and the Northern Rockies*, and his wildlife photography was widely published. (USDA.)

Sam Lee's sister Lena Lee was born July 23, 1885, in Tehama, California, to Que Lee and Shee Chin. In 1903, Lena (left) married Charles Yue (right), who delivered mining supplies from Marysville, California. Charlie was a licensed gold buyer and sold to the San Francisco Mint. In 1899, he operated the Shanghai Restaurant and Bar located in Auburn, California, where Sam Lee settled. (Auburn Joss House Museum.)

Ti Quay Gee (Ti Wung), born on March 14, 1888, in Yreka, California, rented a room at the Quong Lee store while working in 1904 as a pruner of peaches and apricots in the orchards of Deer Creek and later at the vineyard on the Stanford Ranch. He became a beloved member of the Fong family, with whom he lived until the age of 96, working as a cook at their family restaurant, Rice Bowl, in Chico, California. (Henry Fong.)

Like many Chinese American women, Rose had several suitors before choosing Marty Yip from Stockton. Pictured is Rose (Sun) Yip, a daughter of Charlie and Sally Sun, born in Los Molinos, California, along with her siblings Ernest "Ernie" Wilbert Sun, Lilly Gujarno, Burton Sun, Earnest Sun, Walter Sun, Violet Sun, and Annie Sun. (Yip family.)

The Yip family left a lasting legacy in America by commercializing lottery games that are still played today. Marty and Rose (Sun) Yip were a dynamic duo in Stockton, where they owned Marty's Shoe store located at 116 East Washington Street and were active in the Cathay Club. They had five children: Walton, Sandra, and Creighton, who are pictured with Marty in this family photograph. (Yip family.)

Pictured at Mineral Lodge, built in 1940, are Albert Git Lee Chan and Florence Ting SooHoo's four daughters, all born at Saint Elizabeth Hospital in Red Bluff. In 1956, Albert relocated to 1286 Pacifica Avenue in San Francisco to join his cousins in a restaurant business venture. Albert died suddenly on December 5, 1960, in Oakland at the age of 45. (Janet Chan.)

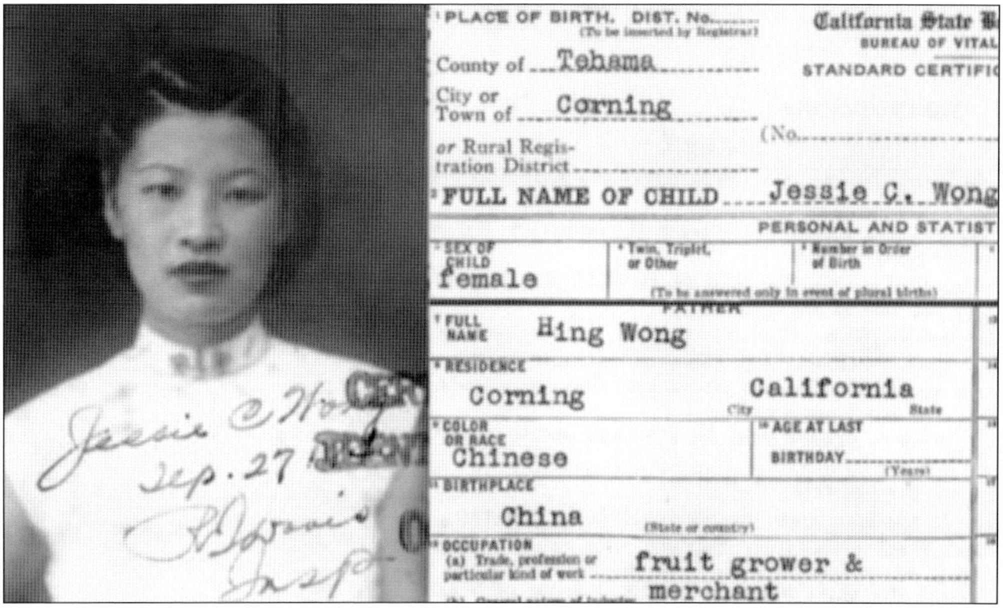

Wong Gum Yow, or Jessie (Wong) Yee, born September 3, 1917, is pictured returning to America on October 18, 1940. She and her siblings were all born in Corning, California, and delivered by Dr. Caroline Howes. Her younger twin siblings, Betty and Jean Wong, were given up for adoption after one month. One went to the paternal side of the Wong family, and the other to the maternal Dong family.

Moon Lim Lee was the former California Department of Transportation (Caltrans) state commissioner and patronized Chinese American businesses along Route 99. He saved the Chinese temple in Weaverville, California, making it a state historic park in September 1956. Pictured from left to right are Helen (Yee) Chew, Chin See, Moon Lee and wife Dorothy, Joe Chew, and Robert Ong.

Grace Darling (Poy) [Yuen] Gan was married to Dr. Chew Owen Yuen until his death in 1954. She worked as a bookkeeper at Supt. Joseph Rapose's office in Red Bluff. She remarried Manville Gan from Los Gatos. Her father, George Poy, was a notable restaurant owner who played a significant role in developing a large Kuomintang chapter in Detroit and hosted Gen. Gee Shong Huey in 1928. (Wei-ling [Yuen] Louie.)

In 1947, the Conard family sold all their parcels in Red Bluff's Chinatown, forcing the Chew family to leave the place where they had first built their life in Red Bluff. Pictured just before its demolition is the Bo Do Hong Company, established in 1865, located at 838 High Street in Red Bluff. This was the last commercial wooden structure to be demolished in Chinatown before the area was redeveloped for large riverfront houses.

Four

Chinese American Veterans

The outbreak of World War II in 1937 brought Chinese immigrants and their descendants even further into mainstream American society. Japan's brutal invasion of China led to greater public sympathy for the Chinese community and prompted Chinese Americans to register for the draft, join war industries, and enlist in record numbers. Of the 13,000 Chinese American soldiers who served during the war, almost half were not US citizens, still barred by the Chinese Exclusion Act of 1882.

Tehama County's non-native-born Chinese- and American-born Chinese became trained pilots and aircrew and fought in ground units for the United States. The wartime labor shortages aided in the repeal of the Chinese Exclusion Act. In 1943, the Magnuson Act ended the ban on naturalization for Chinese immigrants and created a quota to allow 105 Chinese people to immigrate annually. The change enabled the Chinese community who served in military service to finally become naturalized US citizens. Another two years later, the War Bride Act allowed non-quota immigration of women married to United States servicemen. However, it would take the amendment of the 1946 Chinese Alien Wives of American Citizens Act to allow Chinese spouses. The most cherished aspects of Chinese culture were finally made possible, enabling families to live together as one household in the United States.

Imagine, during the Chinese Exclusion Act, which was signed into federal law in 1882 and lasted until 1943, one could not sponsor their family, and as a result, over time, there were very few women of Chinese descent in the United States, furthering the population decline. As Red Bluff became the last Chinatown in Tehama County, their sons were not only proud to serve their country, but many would enlist, send letters, and photographs to keep the community and potential suitresses informed. The young Chinese American women of Tehama County had many suitors sharing these lovely images.

On March 7, 1947, eleven of Red Bluff's Chinese American women held a tea banquet fundraiser for the Second Sino-Japanese War (1937–1945) at the Chew Yuen Company in Red Bluff. From left to right are (first row) Helen Yuen, Helen Foey, Sonny Yuen, Hazel (Chew) Wong, and Hazel (Yuen) Toy; (second row) Annie (Foey) Wong, Mabel On, Julia Chew, Nettie (Chew) Ong, and Violet (Chew) Dong; (third row) Frances (Bo Do Hong) Po-Wen Huang, and Grace (Poy) [Yuen] Gan.

In 1940, Japanese warplanes raided Swatow (Shantou), China, where Frances and her husband were living. Frances returned to Red Bluff and became well-regarded for her community activism and solidarity in the face of a devastating war. Letitia Frances Bo Do Hong married Po Wen Huang (Baldwin Huang), who worked for the Interior of China nationalist government. (Wei-ling [Yuen] Louie.)

In 1938, China's first woman aviatrix ace pilot, Lee Ya-Ching, toured America, fundraising $7 million for the United China Relief campaign. She previously fundraised $3 million for relief work in China. Pictured from left to right are (first row) Hazel (Yuen) Toy, Helen Yuen, and Nettie (Chew) Ong; (second row) Chew Fish Yuen, Chew Owen Yuen, Dr. Chew Yuen, Lee Ya-Ching, Eddie Fong, Violet (Chew) Dong, and Chew Cahoone Yuen.

While serving their country, many received photographs. Mee Ning Fong (Fong Ming Ning) wrote to childhood neighbor Julia Chew. Seen from left to right are Richard Lee (Oakland), Herbert Louie (Sacramento), Peter Gee, Ed Fong, and Mee Ning Fong (Red Bluff); (second row) William Louie, Quok B. Louie, Joe Quan, Howe Lee, and Edmund Fong (Sacramento); (third row) Herbert Quan, David Louie, John Wong, Wing Tow Jue (Sacramento), and George Wing.

Under the Chinese Alien Wives of American Citizens Act, Albert Git Lee Chan had a traditional wedding in China, marrying Florence Ting SooHoo on March 28, 1947. By July 14, 1947, they voyaged to America on the SS *General Gordon* steamship and started their family in Mineral, California. (Courtesy of Janet Chan.)

CLASS "A" PASS
FOR ENLISTED MEN
OF
CAMP HOOD, TEXAS

NAME ______ Git L. ______ RANK ______

Organization ______

ASN ______ Wgt. 125 Hair Blk Eyes ______

is authorized to be absent from Camp Hood, Texas, when off duty between retreat and reveille on week days and from retreat on Saturday to reveille on Monday.

This pass expires ______.

Approved:

[illegible] ADJUTANT [illegible] UNIT COMMANDER

Subject to Rules on Reverse Side of This Pass

Albert Git Lee Chan served in the US Army from March 6, 1943, until 1946. On February 25, 1944, in Camp Hood, Texas, Albert petitioned for naturalization as a US citizen. However, in 1965, his cousins Chin Sue and Wong Kuo Sun were under investigation for deportation under the false claim that Chin Moy was their father. Albert died before the investigation began. (Janet Chan.)

Joe You Chew was drafted into the US Army and stationed at Camp Beale. He was extremely fortunate to be stationed at the recruiting office, where he would make lifelong friends. Based on his bookkeeping skills from his family's restaurant, Joe was later transferred to the finance department. Joe received a Chinese American World War II Veteran Congressional Gold Medal posthumously in 2021.

Joe You Chew brought many suitors to Red Bluff to meet his sisters, nieces, and cousins. His niece Hazel married Robert Wong from Santa Rosa, California. Pictured at Lassen Volcanic National Park in California are, from left to right, (first row) Robert Yuen, Tim Chu, Sam Lowe, Harry Tong, and Edward Chew; (second row) Violet (Chew) Dong, Janie (Chew) Jung, Hazel (Chew) Wong, and Julia Chew; (third row) Robert Wong and Nettie (Chew) Ong.

Chew Fish Yuen is pictured on the left with an unidentified person and Joe You Chew. Fish attended the US Army's language school, learned Mandarin, and became an interpreter. After the US Army, he authored *Chinese Shorthand*, a book still used today for linguistics master's programs. He also authored *Chinese Medicine for the 21st Century.*

After Pvt. Chew Cahoone Yuen landed in the Philippines, the soldiers experienced sniper combat with the Japanese soldiers, followed by a typhoon on the seventh day and air raids over the next few weeks. Cahoone frequently wrote for the *Red Bluff Daily Newspaper* to keep the community informed, sometimes sending sketches to illustrate his experiences. Cahoone (right) was stationed at the US Sixth Army base in New Guinea.

Chew Le-ren Yuen enlisted in the US Air Force for four years, during which time the Vietnam War was being fought, affecting the lives of many young men. He was the first son of Grace (Poy) [Yuen] Gan and Dr. Chew Owen Yuen, born in Red Bluff on September 16, 1946, and passed away on August 7, 2001. (Wei-ling [Yuen] Louie.)

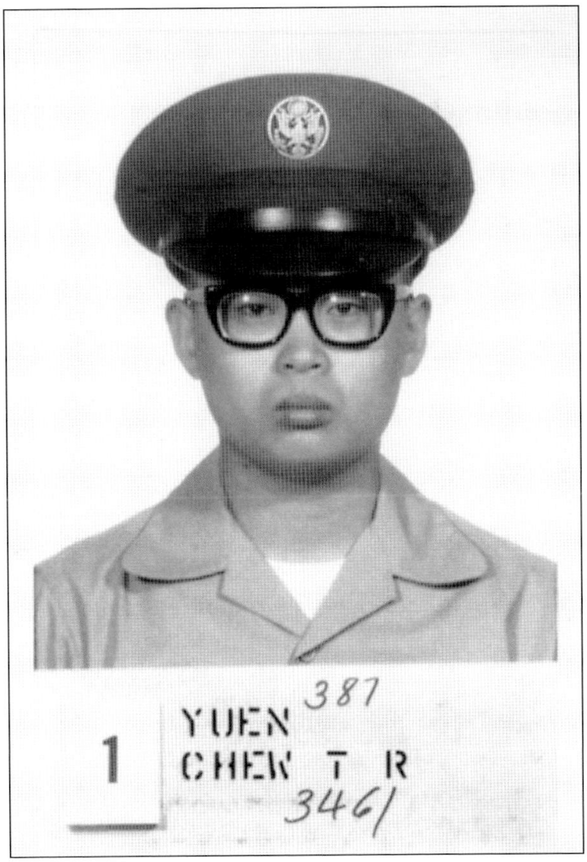

Chew Ty-ren Yuen served in the US Air Force and the 129th Air National Guard. He worked at the NASA Ames Wind Tunnel and retired after 20 years. He was the second son of Grace (Poy) [Yuen] and Dr. Chew Owen Yuen, born in Red Bluff on November 6, 1950, and passed away on September 3, 2011. (Wei-ling [Yuen] Louie.)

During World War II, Henry Chin served in the US Sixth Army for almost three years in the Pacific theater, where he was an auto mechanic. In 1945, Henry was stationed at several different posts in the Philippines, including Lingayen Gulf, Calasiao, San Miguel, San Fernando, San Augustine, and Guimba, Nueva Ecija. Henry received a Chinese American World War II Veteran Congressional Gold Medal posthumously in 2021. (Chin family.)

After a fire broke out in March 1945, employer and landlord Robert Conard provided lodging for the Fong family at the Tremont Hotel while he renovated the brick structure. The Fong family named all of their children after Robert Conard's children, including Chew Mong (Edward) Fong, pictured here, born in 1931 at the Stalker Maternity Home and lived at 831 High Street. He served in the US Air Force as a navigator during the Korean War. (Robert Fong.)

Robert Fong was born on October 29, 1933, at the Stalker Maternity Home. He served in the US Army from 1956 until 1958 as a helicopter mechanic. Bailey Fong was the last one born in Red Bluff. He served in the Reserve.

Nora Chan Marries Harry Fong

At home in Sacramento after a honeymoon trip which included visits to Monterey, Carmel, San Simeon and San Francisco, are the newly wed Mr. and Mrs. Harry G. Fong.

The former Nora C. Chan and Fong were married in the St. Johns Lutheran Church and greeted guests at a reception in the Eagles Hall.

The bride wore a floor length gown of lace over satin with a chapel length train. Sequins and seed pearls accented the Sabrina neckline and tiers of scalloped ruffles formed the bouffant skirt. Her fingertip length veil was held in place by a jeweled headpiece. A white orchid surrounded by carnations and stephanotis formed the bridal bouquet.

Mrs. Florence Fong of Stockton, the bride's sister, was the matron of honor in a lavender satin sheath dress with an over-

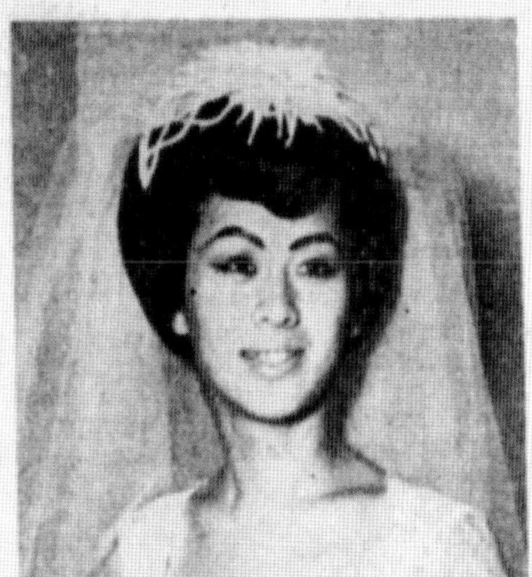

Eddie and Ruby Gee Fong's son Eddie Fong served in the US Army. Their son Harry Fong served in the Navy.

Russell Wong Foey is the last living veteran born in Tehama County. He served in the US Army Signal Corps from 1970 until 1973. He attended basic training at Fort Gordon, Georgia. He was stationed in Germany to work on radio antennas, handling the relay and breakdown of signals. In 2007, Russell and his brother William showcased their love for the outdoors, hunting a prized tule bull elk and later trophy antelope in 2011. (William and Russell Wong Foey.)

Joseph On lived in Reno, Nevada, and served in the US Army. After Joe's father, Frank On, passed away, Joe lived with his mom, Mrs. Lee On, at his sister Mabel (On) Wong's home located at 204 Main Street, Red Bluff, where Joe also lived before being drafted. (Courtesy of William and Russell Wong Foey.)

Pvt. Sammie Foey (right) was awarded an American Theater Ribbon, Good Conduct Medal, and the World War II Victory Medal. Sammie enlisted in the US Army and was stationed as part of the 1006th Second Engineer Flying Training Squadron, AAF (Army Air Force)–AFS (Air Force Station) Barr 47th Squad B, La Junta, Colorado. He worked as an airplane and auto mechanic for the Second Engineer Flying Squadron. He was discharged as a staff sergeant and is pictured here with Herbert (left).

Herbert Foey served his country as a technician fifth grade (TEC 5) in the US Army during World War II and later continued his service in the US Army Medical Service Corps. (Stan Foey and Lisa Sugar.)

Frank Russell Foey was born on August 29, 1930, in Red Bluff. Frank served in the US Army Armed Forces from April 1951 to January 1953 at Fort Ord, California, during the Korean War. He received a letter of appreciation from the Republic of Korea along with a Korean War Service Medal. Frank married Elizabeth "Liz" Joe and settled in Sacramento, California, where they raised three children. (Patty Foey.)

Dave Foey fought in the Battle of the Bulge and helped in the liberation of the Jewish concentration camps. He was born on June 25, 1926, in Red Bluff and served as a tank destroyer driver in the 2nd Armored Battalion attached to General Patton's Third Army 71st Infantry Division during World War II. After the war, he settled in Sacramento and married Helen Leong. (Stan Foey and Lisa Sugar.)

ƆOPER, O., PADDEN, W., SCHOLZ, E., NEWTON, R., BASEY, D., CRIPPEN, L., JOHNSON, A., LUND, Z.
ƆLLARD, J., LUKENS, P., ELWOOD, T., SMITH, P., COOK, G., CLARKE, P., CLARKE, P., MARSHALL, C
RIGHT, JIM, (cook)

ƆTTOM ROW L - R

AMSEY, R., OY, D., CRESS, G., MORRILL, R., MEILI, H., BRAZIE, J., KESTER, WM., LINDLAND, J.,
LARKE, W., BRYCE, P., ROWLEY, C., BOUCHER, A., BANTO, L., NEWBERRY, BOB

The most notable veteran is decorated war hero Danny On, the first Asian Pacific American Forest Service smokejumper. He served as a paratrooper in the 101st Airborne Division during World War II in the 1944 Battle of the Bulge in Bastogne, Belgium. (Siskiyou Smokejumper Base Museum.)

Danny On received two Purple Hearts, one Bronze Star, and, posthumously, in 2021, a Chinese American World War II Veteran Congressional Gold Medal. The Siskiyou Smoke Jumper Museum proudly highlights Danny's legacy. (Siskiyou Smoke Jumper Museum.)

Five

Cantonese American Funeral Processions

Segregation in America resulted in Chinese cemeteries typically being located at the rear or as a distinctly marked section. Some still have 19th-century brick-oven structures where the deceased's belongings were burned and offerings such as roasted pig were left to nourish the spirit of the dead. It is widely known that vagrants would steal these offerings. In Chinese culture, it is customary for those who die overseas to be temporarily buried while waiting to be exhumed and then reburied in their ancestral plot. Before interment, the bones were typically scrubbed, cleaned, and then shipped to China so that the soul rests more easily on home ground. For some, after 1949, they could not intern the bodies in China. For those laborers who had employment agreements, the Tong (agencies) were responsible for gathering their remains. Red Bluff has the most burials, with many living beyond 80 years old. In Chinese culture, longevity is a feat worth celebrating since the belief is that one's life has been lived to the fullest with no desires left to be fulfilled.

For each of the five original families who decided to make America their home, and with the passing of each family clan, they held an old country Cantonese funeral procession to the gravesite. They first took the deceased to visit all their favorite places in Chinatown, with old Chinese folk music played during the procession. For those families who converted to Christianity, the gravesite was blessed before the arrival of the deceased. A going-away party with a Cantonese meal was held at the family's home because all must be happy for their longevity and celebration of life. At home, firecrackers and loud music ward off evil spirits that might be lingering. The family gives guests a red-and-white envelope with a coin and lucky candy, which should not be taken home because it is believed to invite bad luck. By eating the candy, one adds sweetness to a bitter occasion, and by spending the coin before returning home, one wards off bad spirits and brings good fortune to others.

Pictured are the descendants who are forever grateful to Lew Jung (Lei Jung, Hei Shoon, or Fong Shew Ming) and May Yuk (Seeto) Jung. Both created a generational legacy from 大井尾 (Dajingwei or Ai Dieng Mei), China, to Willows, California, by sponsoring the immigration of many and providing employment at their businesses. (Lew and Fong families.)

While the Chinese community in Vina may be gone, their legacy lives on through the vineyards they helped build and maintain. Today, all that remains is this oven, which was last used by one of the original Chinese families in Tehama County for Joe You Chew. From left to right are William Foey, Argel Sabillo, Bruce Chin, and Jessica (Casas) Chew (next to the burner), Jack Thompson, and Mitchel and Tamara Kofford.

Dr. Chu Suey Gee, born in 1877, frequently traveled from San Francisco to Red Bluff. When he died in 1955, a traditional Chinese funeral procession traveled through the streets of San Francisco's Chinatown. From left to right are (first row) Violet (Chew) Dong, Julia Chew, Rose SooHoo, Jane (Chew) Jung, and Nettie (Chew) Ong; (second row) Chew Cahoone Yuen, Joe You Chew, Emmet Pendleton, Chew Fish Yuen, Edward Chew, and Dr. Chu Suey Gee.

Charlie Cone, born in 1868, was a beloved person at the Cone Ranch and a fondly remembered by many, including prominent political leaders such as Douglas Spencer, Marie Cone, and Anna Reppert Cone. As a result, he was not buried in the segregated Chinese Section at Oak Hill Cemetery in Red Bluff but rather in Joseph Cone's wife's family plot. His pallbearers were William Foey, Eddie Fong, James Fong, Charlie Long, Yee Sing, and Kim Sing.

黄 (Wong) Shuy was known as Charlie Kimball, born in 1849 and died on November 17, 1912. His employer, Gorham Gates Kimball, held a deep affection for Wong, as they frequently traveled together. When Kimball passed away, Wong inherited $500, a watch, and a chain. Kimball's nephew Gorham King made sure that Wong received a proper burial within the King family plot. Wong not only spoke English but could also read and write.

Although during the 19th century, Chinese immigrants faced much discrimination and were not permitted to buy graveyard plots in many regions, this was not the case in Tehama County. Many are buried in owned plots. Seto QiChang, who is from Kaping Jinji Taishan Kaiping, China (欽牛肉奇陽里, 御其昌公之墓, 開平縣 金氣水), is buried in the Chinese Section at Oak Hill Cemetery in Red Bluff. (Chinese characters courtesy of Qi Li.)

This 19th-century Chinese Section has been in continuous use since the arrival of Chinese immigrants. Ms. Sinu from Kaiping County (大南村人, 奥四女公之墓, 開平赤坎) is buried in the Chinese Section next to Mr. Qi Chiang from Kaiping County (欽牛肉奇陽里, 御其昌公之墓,開平縣 金氣水) at Oak Hill Cemetery in Red Bluff. (Chinese characters courtesy of Qi Li.)

There are many old, unmarked gravestones with headstones that have been removed. It is unclear how many graves are within the Chinese Section at Oak Hill Cemetery in Red Bluff. This headstone, located in Oak Hill Cemetery in Red Bluff, bears a traditional Cantonese inscription reading "Tomb of Ao Zhuhai from Zhushan Village, Kaiping County" (竹門村, 奥柱海公之墓, 開平縣). (Chinese characters courtesy of Qi Li.)

While the location of the early Chinese graves is unknown, the Helen and Joe Chew Foundation has initiated a series of conservation projects for the near future to restore the existing headstones and add a memorial. 長安村, 黃門林氏之墓, 台山縣 Wong Nee Lim (Lim Shee) is buried in Oak Hill Cemetery, Red Bluff, California. This traditional headstone ensures the resting place is not just a grave but also a record of heritage, culture, and history that connects the past to future generations. (Chinese characters courtesy of Qi Li.)

In 2022, the remaining descendants of Tehama County started coordinating 清明节 (Qingming) in an effort to save their deteriorating historic Chinese Section, where many notable and prominent early Chinese leaders are buried. Discovered in the Oak Hill Cemetery's office, these headstones commemorate individuals from Xikuo Village (台山) and Leung Village (西廓) in Taishan County, Guangdong, preserving their ancestral ties and village identities for descendants. (Chinese characters courtesy of Qi Li.)

Gene Fong (馮) is the grandson of Gin "Charlie" Fong and is buried at the edge of the Chinese Section at the Oak Hill Cemetery in Red Bluff. Gin Fong was known as Charlie Ramsay and worked for the Cone Ranch and the T.H. Ramsay family in Battle Creek, California, in the 1860s. He remained the family cook until his death in March 1956.

黄德純翁墓 (Wong Foey, or Wong Duk Shun) was born in April 1849 in Tianxin Village (田心村) and died on December 12, 1912, at the age of 63, one week shy of his son Tang Foey's arranged marriage. In his final years, he recounted his life with his daughter Maybelle (Foey) Woo. He had a Cantonese funeral, celebrating his life with rituals at his store; the family hired a procession band from San Francisco and whalers to mourn while walking in the hearse from Chinatown to Oak Hill Cemetery. (Wong family.)

Julia Jue Foey (Julia Wong Foey) encouraged her daughters to play musical instruments, although she held little value for higher education. She was Wong Foey's second wife and had bound feet. Although Julia's headstone states that she was born in 1877, her obituary had her year of birth as 1873. This type of discrepancy was not unusual due to the challenging immigration process.

Since 黄 George Kim Poy Foey died before his parents, a wake was held at Wong Foey's residence. In alignment with Chinese tradition, it is required that a child be buried in silence. George was born on February 2, 1906, as the fourth child of Wong Foey's second marriage. He died on January 25, 1921, after being treated for tuberculosis in Colfax.

黄 Tang Kim (Wong) Foey was born in 1889 and died in 1960. His father, Wong Foey, held high expectations for him, and in his youthful years, he worked for his father at Quong Ying Low Company as a salesclerk and various other jobs, including at the Vestal Meat Market. He eventually became the proprietor of Golden Eagle Café with his cousin Henry Yuen in 1917.

易 Yee Yat or Yat Hang Foey originally had bound feet but was able to reverse the binding through a painful process. She had an arranged marriage to Tang Foey. Her father, 易 Dum Yee, was the principal of the Chinese school located at 907-913 Third Street in Sacramento, California, and taught his daughter several Chinese dialects.

On March 19, 1938, a canoe capsized in the Sacramento River. While Danny On survived, Albert Foey tragically drowned at the age of 16. 黄 Albert (Wong) Foey was the sixth of fourteen children born to Tang and Yat Foey and was born on June 12, 1921. Albert was a member of the Red Bluff High School C Basketball Team.

Herbert (Wong) Foey was 黄 Tang and Yat Foey's eighth of fourteen children and was born on November 9, 1923, in Red Bluff and died on March 6, 1998. After serving in the US Army during World War II, he found a new career as an accountant and settled in Sacramento.

黄 Henry L. (Wong) Foey was the thirteenth of fourteen children born to Tang and Yat Foey. He was born on November 18, 1933, in Red Bluff and died on October 16, 2001. After he served in the US Army, he settled in Sacramento in 1951 and worked as a foreman for the US Postal Service.

黄 Wing (Wong) Foey (Herbert Wing Foey or Kim Foey) was born in 1907 and died in 1938 of lockjaw. His nickname was "Hobo Foey" because he enjoyed hunting, gambling, riding freight trains, and hitchhiking. Although he lived an unconventional lifestyle, he was a colorful person and even considered a favorite uncle in his family.

黄 William Clifford (Wong) Foey was the youngest child of Wong Foey and Julia Foey, born at 824 High Street in Red Bluff. William was a cook at the Tremont Hotel. After selling his father's Corning property, he opened Bill's Diner, located on Main and Sycamore Streets. He then moved to 534 Oak Street until his home was taken by eminent domain for $20,000 to build the Tehama County Jail.

Betty Ming (Woo) Foey was William Wong Foey's first wife. Betty died shortly after their daughter Sharon Foey was born on October 9, 1941, from birth complications. Betty was born in 1922 in China to Mr. and Mrs. James Woo of Los Angeles, California. Betty immigrated at three months old, and her siblings were Howard, Henry, Frank, Mary, and Amy Woo.

William Clifford Foey remarried Mabel Anna On, born in Red Bluff on November 30, 1926, and died June 30, 1992. Their two sons, Russell and William Wong Foey, became the last residents to live in Tehama County from the Foey and On family tree. (William and Russell Wong Foey.)

Lew Qwon On, otherwise widely known as Frank On, was born in 1889 and died in 1950. His wife, Mrs. Lee You On, outlived him by 23 years. Following Frank's death, Mrs. Lee You On had to navigate the probate process to secure her late husband's shares in a modest Hong Kong estate. (William and Russell Wong Foey.)

Mrs. Lee You On, born on November 1, 1895, was the matriarch of the On household. She was exceptional at making business decisions, financing a credit system at their restaurant, and showing equality to Native American patrons. When she died on October 22, 1973, her family honored her wishes to have an old country Cantonese funeral with a procession. (William and Russell Wong Foey.)

After Danny On, pictured second from the upper right, died in 1979, his friends championed the US Department of Agriculture's creation of the Danny On Memorial Hiking Trail No. 370 in Whitefish, Montana. Danny On is the most notable Chinese American veteran born on May 11, 1924, in Red Bluff. He died in a skiing accident. (Siskiyou Smoke Jumper Museum.)

廣東省 台山縣, 陳想華翁之墓, 六村鄉 大湾村 Henry Chin was an auto mechanic at various dealerships in Red Bluff before retiring from the Sacramento Police Department. Born on September 26, 1920, he died on October 3, 1999. At his request, his children honored him by burying him with his son Randall. (Chin family.)

廣東省台山縣, 陳門趙氏麗瑜之墓, 浮石鄉,第七村 Lai Chew was born on August 6, 1927, and died on October 5, 2008. At her request, she also desired to be buried with her son Randall (October 27, 1948–February 14, 1949). (Chin family.)

趙綏賢公之墓, 浮石村 Dr. Chew Yuen (front right) was a man whose accomplishments still command great respect among those who knew the Chew family. Dr. Chew Yuen passed away in 1947. Before he passed away, he built two roads and created a second tomb for himself in Fow Shek Village, Guangdong Province, China.

浮石村 , 趙母梁氏安人墓, 台山縣 The union of Dr. Chew Yuen and Wong Shee (left) created multiple generations of Chinese American doctors. Their four sons upheld the legacy of the Chew Yuen Company, mastering the art of Traditional Chinese Medicine until 1983. Even though their father's surname was Chew, all of Dr. Chew Yuen's American-born children became known as Yuen.

Wong Shee and Dr. Chew Yuen's first child was 趙 Dr. Chew Robert Yuen (Robert Bo Do Hong or Too Suey Wee), born on November 8, 1907, in Red Bluff's white neighborhood and died May 13, 1991. He attended St. Mary's College and then operated a Traditional Chinese Medicine practice on Chestnut Street, Mount Shasta, California; he was frequently accused of practicing without a license. Pictured left to right are Won Chew, Robert Chew, and Violet (Chew) Dong.

Pictured from left to right are (first row) Theodore Yuen, Linda Yuen, Emily (Louis) Yuen, and Patricia Yuen; (second row) Stanford Chew Yuen, Robert Chew Yuen Jr., Dr. Chew Robert Yuen; Emily married Robert on June 6, 1928, at the Presbyterian church in Red Bluff with hundreds of guests wearing their best Cheongsam. Emily was the daughter of Mr. and Mrs. Louie Bow from Walnut Grove. (Wei-ling [Yuen] Louie.)

趙公信偉之墓 Dr. Chew Owen Yuen was born on June 22, 1915, at 202-204 Walnut Street in Red Bluff. He was Wong Shee and Dr. Chew Yuen's second-born son. He was considered an all-American athlete and named after Dr. Joseph Allen Owen Sr. from Axtel Breckinridge County, Kentucky. He was the first of Dr. Chew Yuen's children to attend college, earning degrees from California State University, Chico, and the California Chiropractic College in Oakland, California.

Dr. Chew Owen Yuen (fourth from left) was the first son to continue his father's Traditional Chinese Medicine practice in Red Bluff. Owen was also accomplished in doubles ping pong, earning the title of champion. He was an active member of several organizations, including the Kiwanis Club, Chiropractic Association, and Badminton Club. Owen passed away unexpectedly on March 1, 1954, and his family held his funeral services at First Presbyterian Church. Pictured at Corning Park, from left to right are Gin, Don, Cahoone, Owen, Kid, and Nettie (Chew) Ong.

浮石村, 趙公仁偉之墓, 台山縣 Dr. Chew Fish Yuen was born on November 14, 1918, at 202-204 Walnut Street, Red Bluff, California. A gifted translator, calligraphy writer, music composer, engineer, and Traditional Chinese Medicine physician, his degrees include DC, ND, AB, BS, MA, and a PHC from Kwangtung, China; University of Nevada-Reno; Columbia University; California Chiropractic College in Oakland; and University of California, Berkeley.

Dr. Chew Fish Yuen (pictured in the center) expanded his family's Traditional Chinese Medicine practice to Santa Rosa and Ukiah in California. He was the Honor Life President of the Chinese Herbal and Acupuncture Association of America, an organization that represents practitioners of Traditional Chinese Medicine in the United States. He made significant contributions by donating his family's artifacts to various Chinese historical societies and museums.

台山縣, 趙公仁偉之墓, 浮石村 Dr. Chew Cahoone Yuen, born on May 23, 1920, at 202-204 Walnut Street in Red Bluff, was a gifted abstract non-objective modern artist featured at the Philbrook Art Center Museum in Tulsa, Oklahoma, Crocker Art Museum, Shasta College, and California State University, Chico. Pictured from left to right are Fish Yuen, Rose SooHoo, Jim Sing Jr., Nettie (Chew) Ong, Jim Chew, Julia Chew, Cahoone Yuen, and Janie (Chew) Jung.

On October 1, 1983, the last generational Traditional Chinese Medicine physician in Northern California died. Cahoone had not only followed in his brothers' footsteps of becoming a physician, but he also researched cancer methods and antibiotics from soil. He attended California State University, Chico, and Los Angeles Chiropractic College and was the secretary of the Biological Research Garden, San Francisco. Dr. Chew Yuen's residence was sold by his wife, Carmen, in 1994.

浮石村, 趙秋鳳 女士墓, 台山縣 Helen Marie Yuen was born on September 27, 1926, at 202-204 Walnut Street in Red Bluff. She became ill after accompanying her sister Letitia Frances Po-Wen Huang (Bo Do Hong) and her father, Dr. Chew Yuen, to the United Chinese Relief Society in San Francisco to meet Madame Chiang Kai-shek. She died suddenly on March 30, 1943, at the Tung Wah Hospital.

Lily Elsie Sun from Willows married Henry Yuen in 1924, but their nuptials ended in divorce by 1925. Three years later, Henry married actress Poon Wai Jing at Mr. and Mrs. Huwai Kee's home, located at 1050 Clay Street in San Francisco. By 1933, Henry married a third time in Seattle, Washington. Their second child, Frank Yuen, was born on September 20, 1935, but died on January 1, 1936.

趙士优 公之墓,台山縣 浮石村 Chew You was one of five brothers born on September 23, 1868, to Chew Hing Quong and Shung Shee. In 1934, Chew You died at 66 years old after a car door slammed on his fingers while attending a funeral, which caused an infection that continued to fester and spread throughout his body. Many people sent money in an effort to save his life.

趙母五有女墓安人墓 台山縣 浮石村 Mrs. Ng Shee Chew was born on May 20, 1881. She found life in America exceedingly difficult, as she had come from relatively comfortable circumstances in China, where girls of her generation were required by tradition to have bound feet. After her husband Chew You died, she worked at the restaurant, becoming prominent in restaurant circles, and passed away on May 11, 1958. Pictured from left to right are (first row) Mrs. Kai and Julia Chew; (second row) Mrs. Bing Kai, Lorena Kai, Janie Chew, Ng Shee, Chin See, Mammie, and Nettie (Chew) Ong.

趙茂麟公之墓, 台山縣 浮石村 Dick Chew was born in 1902 and died in 1971. Many mourned him. His pallbearers were Chew, Cahoone Yuen, Gene Hing, Sammie Foey, Walter Irey, Jim Davis, Ralph Ehorn, Loren Forward, Bernard Bosse, F.B. Godbolt, Herb Viears, Jim Froome Jr., Melvin Wells, Max Stewart, and Don Phillips. From left to right are (first row) William Chu and Dick Chew; (second row) Edward Chew, Lai (Chew) Chin, Helen Yee, and Joe Chew.

趙母陈 順 蘭 安人墓台山縣 浮石村 Chin See (Suon Lon Chin), was born in 1902 and passed away in February 1967 after being diagnosed with cancer. On her deathbed, she told Joe You Chew, "The restaurant business will kill you." The Chew family sold the Ming Terrace Restaurant in 1973. From left to right are Julia Chew, Chin See, Edward Chew, Curtis Chew, May (Wong) Chew, Gerald Chew, and Dick Chew.

趙菲華之墓, 台山縣 浮石村 Julia Chew was born at the Bo Do Hong Company on July 18, 1924, located at 838 High Street in Red Bluff. Pictured from left to right are Chin See, Ng Shee, Nettie (Chew) Ong, Dick Chew, Julia Chew, Ned Chew, Violet (Chew) Dong, and Joe Chew. She died on September 14, 2014. Julia's love for taking pictures resulted in some of the only pictures of Red Bluff's Chinatown.

趙晉豪台山縣 浮石村 Edward Chew was born on October 28, 1926, at the Bo Do Hong Company, located at 838 High Street in Red Bluff, to Dick Chew and Chin See. Edward loved working as a cook at the Ming Terrace Restaurant and wanted to keep the family business. After the restaurant was sold, he enjoyed trying other family-operated Chinese American restaurants, requesting that they overcook the vegetables. From left to right are Edward Chew, Robert Chin (in foreground), Sam Lowe, Tim Chu, Harry Low, Joe Chew, and Robert Wong.

趙鄧美寶氏之墓 The wife of Joe Chew, Helen Mable (Yee) Chew, is pictured in the middle of the second row with her coworkers at the California Department of Water Resources, located in Red Bluff. Helen was born on July 14, 1924, in Phoenix, Arizona, to Toy Sleung Yee and Mah Shee, who operated the Toy Sleung Yee Grocery store after a failed laundry venture in Boston. She died on June 22, 2013.

趙壽麟公之墓, 台山縣浮石村 Joe You Chew was the longest-living Chinese American to ever reside in Tehama County, reaching the age of 99 years old. He labeled the photographs in this book. Pictured from left to right are (first row) Diane Chew, Joe Chew, Jessica (Casas) Chew, and Dr. Kenneth Chew; (second row) Edward and Calvin Tang, Jonathan and Karen (Kwok) Chew, May (Wong) Chew, Argel Sabillo, Eric Chew, and Barbara (Fong) Chew.

Following the death of Joe You Chew, the Chinese American descendants of Red Bluff, California, helped the Helen and Joe Chew Foundation champion the "Historic Chinatown Alley" street naming with the help of HAPI (Humboldt Asians & Pacific Islanders in Solidarity) and the support of the Red Bluff City Council and Planning Department. The alleyway now looks down upon the Chinatown that was once so vibrant and cherished in the hearts of many families across America, unveiling Red Bluff's beautiful Chinese American history.

趙晋德台山縣浮石村 By the 20th century, Dr. Kenneth Kendall Chew revolutionized the science of shellfish and aquaculture. In 2014, the US National Oceanic and Atmospheric Administration named a building the Kenneth K. Chew Center for Shellfish Research and Restoration, located in Clam Bay, Manchester, Washington. Pictured from left to right are Curtis Chew, Matthew Chew, May (Wong) Chew, Kenneth Chew, Marcella Chew, and Gerald Chew.

As a dedication to the last Chinatown Pioneer of Tehama County, signs were installed on the late Dr. Kenneth Kendall Chew's birthday on October 29, 2022. It marked the end of an era. Pictured from left to right are Mayor Chad Parker, Daniele Eyestone, Andrew, Bruce Chin, Jessica (Casas) Chew, Mayor Karen Deiters, Steve Piffero, Argel Sabillo, Russell Wong Foey, William Wong Foey, Alden Cruz, Dave Gowan, and Tom Westbrook.

About the Organization

The Helen and Joe Chew Foundation (HJC) was started by three alumni from the University of San Francisco, all of whom are driven by their compassion for others. The HJC president and founder, Jessica, is the only grandchild of Helen and Joe Chew. From an early age, she was aware of the significance her Chew family legacy had on the Red Bluff community. When her grandfather turned 99 years old, she began reviewing some of his work. To her surprise, he had been creating binders that contained sleeve protectors of family letters, newspaper clippings, memorial service programs, and, most importantly, photographs that he had labeled with the help of his nephew Bruce Chin. As Jessica and Bruce recounted some of his life's stories, they realized the magnitude of his friendships, with many inspiring individuals he had known in his lifetime. The accomplishments of not only his family but also his friends were astonishing. With the help of her cousin Bruce Chin, Argel Sabillo, and Alden Cruz, the four of them spearheaded HJC's mission to support higher education while preserving Tehama County's rich Chinese American history, fulfilling one of Joe's last wishes from his granddaughter. The objective of this book is to reconstruct the descendants' loving memories in order to share their origin stories and to continue to search for the descendants of Tehama County.

Discover Thousands of Local History Books Featuring Millions of Vintage Images

Arcadia Publishing, the leading local history publisher in the United States, is committed to making history accessible and meaningful through publishing books that celebrate and preserve the heritage of America's people and places.

Find more books like this at
www.arcadiapublishing.com

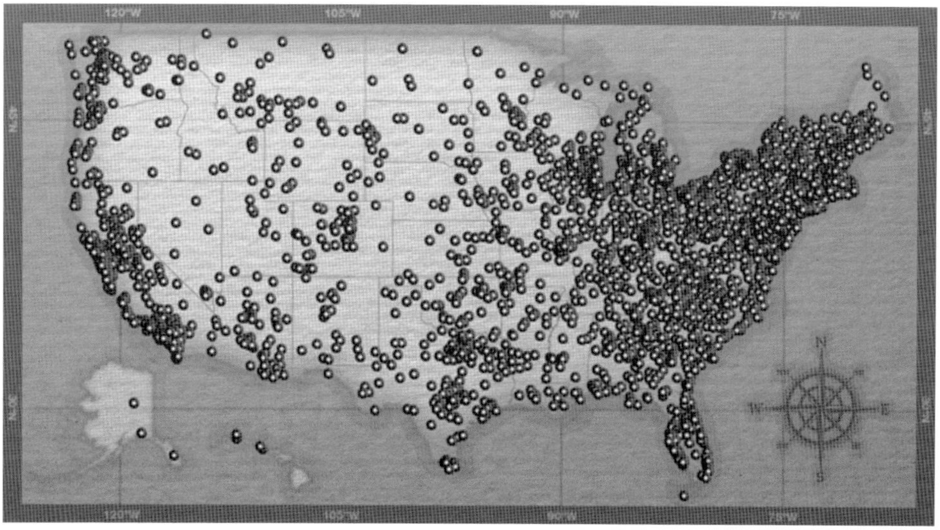

Search for your hometown history, your old stomping grounds, and even your favorite sports team.

Consistent with our mission to preserve history on a local level, this book was printed in South Carolina on American-made paper and manufactured entirely in the United States. Products carrying the accredited Forest Stewardship Council (FSC) label are printed on 100 percent FSC-certified paper.

MADE IN THE USA